THE GUIDED AUTHOR

A leader's practical guide to
go from idea to a published book
in a few months

MOUSTAFA HAMWI

PASSIONPRENEUR®
PUBLISHING

Publishing information
Publishing, design, and production facilitated by Passionpreneur Publishing, A division of Passionpreneur Organization Pty Ltd, ABN: 48640637529

www.PassionpreneurPublishing.com
Melbourne, VIC | Australia

WHAT GLOBAL LEADERS ARE SAYING ABOUT MOUSTAFA

"Moustafa is one of the great 100 Leaders and Coaches of the future."

— DR MARSHALL GOLDSMITH
WORLD'S #1 EXECUTIVE COACH

"Moustafa…Mr. Passion!"

— THE LATE PROF. TONY BUZAN
INVENTOR OF MIND MAPPING, NOBEL PEACE PRIZE NOMINEE

"One of the few individuals that truly understands the power of passion and is making a real difference in the world."

— JOHN MATTONE
WORLD'S #1 AUTHORITY ON INTELLIGENT LEADERSHIP

"If I can give you one piece of advice: if you lack passion, call Moustafa!"

— FONS TROMPENAARS
WORLD'S LEADING AUTHORITY ON CORPORATE CULTURE

TO DR. MARSHALL GOLDSMITH

*You inspired my thought leadership journey and
gave me the insights needed to develop
the Guided Author System.*

*I owe a big part of my success as an international
author, and a publisher, to you.*

FOREWORD

BY DR. MARSHALL GOLDSMITH

WHY WRITE A BOOK?

If you want to leave a legacy and have a message to share with the world, write a book!

Writing a book is one of the greatest tools of thought leadership that an executive can have. Through this book, *The Guided Author*, Moustafa Hamwi gives a practical process for creating a book for busy leaders who have the subject matter expertise but are not professional writers.

WANT TO WRITE A GOOD BOOK? GET HELP!

You might have heard of my three best-selling books: *Mojo*, *Triggers*, and *What Got You Here Won't Get You There*. All three are New York Times bestsellers, but I did not write any of those books by myself. I got help!

Now, those books are incredibly well-written, and I can say that without bragging. Why? I didn't write them. My strength is in ideas. So, I come up with ideas, record them, and my writing partner and I then work together. This is part of what inspired the recording process in *The Guided Author System.*

Although I am an excellent writer, my writing partner is much better than me. I could not have written any of those books by myself.

Yes, as a successful executive and thought leader, you may have great content. But can you write? Writing is hard! Good writing is incredibly difficult. If you're not a great writer, use a structured system, or find a market-leading professional who can be your writing partner. *The Guided Author* opens the door to both.

THREE THINGS SUCCESSFUL PEOPLE DO, AND YOU NEED THEM TO FINISH YOUR BOOK!

From my experience coaching some of the world's best leaders, including 150 of the Fortune 500 companies, I have discovered something: what makes the most highly successful leaders different is also what makes them some of the greatest leaders in history. I believe there are three characteristics that differentiate good leaders from great leaders. They are:

- Courage. Great leaders have the courage to get feedback and to look at themselves in the mirror, honestly. This isn't an easy task. To truly look at yourself and to ask for, accept, and act on feedback you receive from others, you have to have courage.
- Humility: You don't have to know all the answers to be a good leader. You must be able to ask for help when you need it.
- Discipline. To be a great leader, you have to have the discipline to follow up and do the hard work to keep getting better.

All three of these represent the core of *The Guided Author System*. So, if you have the courage to share your message with the world through a book, and the humility to seek help on that journey, then Moustafa is your best bet. I love working with him. He is positive, he is passionate, he is committed, and he loves what he is doing.

All that is left for you to find is the discipline to follow through with *The Guided Author System* and share your book with the world.

Dr. Marshall Goldsmith
Thinker50 #1 Executive Coach
4X New York Times bestselling author

CONTENTS

ACKNOWLEDGMENTS

Iowe a big thank you to a lot of people who helped this book see the light. Below, I list only a few, simply because I would need a full book to acknowledge them all.

To the souls of real men who left a legacy of thought leadership in this world:

- Firstly, to the soul of my late father for having one of the highest levels of commitment and work ethics I have ever seen, even when on his death bed. It inspired me to finish writing this book one week after his passing.
- To the late Prof. Tony Buzan, for honouring me with the title 'Mr Passion' and for the valuable contribution Mind Mapping has had on my life.

To my mom and sisters for supporting me to finish this book during the mourning period after dad passed away – you are the kind of women that make a real man.

To my best friends and their families* for being there for me in my darkest moments. I could have not made it without you:

- Abdel-Moneim Khalil,
- Bassem Tirkawi,
- Taj Khayat.

To the supportive friends* that made my move to Australia a great experience:

- Abdulhameed Qawasmi,
- Allan Pease,
- Basel Dabbagh,
- Ian Cariaga,
- Khalida Jawadi,
- Patrick Begg,
- Said Saadi,
- Sofia Neale,
- Yaser Dabbagh,
- Yas Matbouli.

To the legendary international authors* who had a profound impact on my journey with your genuine care in every interaction we had:

- Brian Tracy,
- Fons Trompenaars,
- Dr. John Demartini,
- Ron Kaufman,
- Sally Helgesen,
- Stephen M. R. Covey.

To my business associates*:

- Gautam Ganglani for the continuous support throughout my journey,
- Graeme Brown for the amazing editorial support,
- Sohin Lakhani for taking the time to review and give feedback on this book while it was in development.

Thanks to my team* that helped me make this book as good as it can be:

- Cat Martindale-Vale for the amazing publishing management,
- Clare McIvor for her support in bringing out the right tone in the book,
- Diane Lucas and Linda Honeysett for keeping our finances in order,
- Franziska Berthold and Charles Tan for the great publishing support,
- Jasmine Hessel for the great mentoring support,
- Lolita Catabui for being my trusted assistant,
- Mohamed Mohsen for the great design support,
- Dr Scott Hurley for being my diligent and trusted editor,
- Sonja Ceri and Jesse Morris for the great marketing support,
- Vinita and Vikas Bhatia for the great digital footprint,
- To the rest of my team at Passionpreneur Publishing who made this book see the light.

And to the whole Passionpreneur Author Tribe, I'm still on this journey because of you.

Finally, to everyone who supported me but I couldn't mention on this page, know that in my heart, I will always appreciate your support.

---

* everyone's name, aside from my family, is mentioned in alphabetical order

INTRODUCTION

AUTHOR = AUTHORITY

Welcome and well done! I'm thrilled that you want to become an international author. I am happy to say you've chosen the right passion tribe to help you on this journey. It is our mission at Passionpreneur Publishing to help inspiring leaders like you share their message and become global thought leaders. Together, we can spread passion and purpose in the world. I promise you this is going to be one of the most rewarding things you ever do in your life.

I'll never forget the day my first book arrived from the printer, and I took it out of the box — it's as close as it gets to having a baby! The product of your hard work, your hopes, your blood, sweat and tears, the object of your pride is now in the world and you are holding it in your hands. What a moment!

I would love to help you feel that same feeling. That's what this book is all about.

You've probably thought for some time that you have a book in you. You've excelled in your career and have kept learning as you moved through the ranks. You've seen what works and what doesn't. You have so much to say about your area of expertise, not just big ideas but practical ones, about how to get things done. But how do you let the world know? How do you even find the time to get it on paper? It's one of the ironies of life that when you're young, you have all the time in the world to write the kind of book you have in you, but you lack the necessary knowledge and experience. Being an experienced leader, you've got so much to say — but where's the time to do it?

That's why I want to dispel the first myth about becoming an author right now: that it has to take a lot of time. It doesn't. The material is in you, it's there; you just need the right method to get it out. This is where most people become stuck. So, this is where I did the work.

I've developed this method the slow and hard way. I was never the sort of person who loved to read, and I sure didn't love to write. I had so much to say, but every time I sat down to get it on paper, nothing came. I couldn't even finish a blog post, never mind write a whole book.

Being relentlessly curious, I set myself the goal of figuring out a way. I spoke to hundreds of published authors in the business and personal development fields. Some of them became mentors. Two things they had in common were being super-organised and very practical. This is something you already know, right? To do a job well, plan, plan, plan. Break the large task into small ones; outline a structure to achieve them, but be flexible enough to improvise as necessary. Allow enough time, but use the time efficiently.

I thought I could just sit down and write an entire book without a plan or a method. No wonder the words wouldn't come! But after speaking to the experts, I saw how I could get it done. So, taking pieces of advice from each of my sources, I got to work — properly this time. Within a month or so, the manuscript for my first book was finished! A few months after that, it had been published.

More books have followed, including this one, none of them taking more than that same few months of thorough preparation and dedicated work to get them ready for publishing. I was so excited by my breakthrough that I started a publishing company for people like me and people like you — busy, working people who have something to say and are passionate about making the world better. Passionpreneur Publishing has worked with more than 100 authors. The great majority of our writers had never published before. Coaching each one of them, sharing their passion, and helping them bring to life the book inside them has been a wonderful journey for me. Each of these experiences has also helped me put together and refine the Guided Author System we use at Passionpreneur.

The book you're reading is the result of all that hard work. The Guided Author System you'll find in these pages is designed to help executives and high-performing leaders become international authors. You do not need to be a writer; you just need to be an expert in your field with something to say and the passion to be a global thought leader. The Guided Author System will help you get all those ideas from your head and onto the pages of your book. It will also optimise your time and effort, allowing you to manage your workload, hit your deadlines and still enjoy the process. In fact, this guide is so systematic and process-oriented that you should really think of it more as a workbook. Simply follow the process outlined in these pages, and you'll have produced your book's content within a month or two. Yes, I mean that. It can be done.

Is that the end of the journey though? Definitely not. There's one other thing first-time authors find as challenging as actually writing their book, and that's navigating the publishing process itself. Our industry is mysterious, and a little intimidating if we are honest. There are thousands of publishers out there. How do you find the right one? How do you prepare your manuscript so that it appeals to publishers in the first place?

The Guided Author has you covered. In these pages, you'll find everything you need to know about what happens *after* you write your book. It's not just about finding a publisher, though that's the most important step. You've got to think about your cover, your title, and even your author photograph. There is publicity to manage, testimonials to get and that ever-important copy for the back cover. My experience publishing transformational books by experts like you has taught me the ins and outs of the business — what to look for, the mistakes to avoid, the best way to maximise your resources, and many other insider tricks. Nearly half of *The Guided Author* is devoted to the publishing leg of your author journey. I've even included a couple of bonus chapters on what happens after publishing.

At Passionpreneur we have a saying, *"It's not about the book, it's about who you become after publishing the book."* I really believe this. Whenever new authors come to us for help to bring their books to life, the first thing we do is talk about the *Why* of their project. *Why* do they want to publish? The majority of these authors are very well-educated; they're usually pretty success-ful in their careers — CXOs, VPs and directors. But some-thing is missing. We know they have something to say and want to share the benefits of their experience with the world. But they also want to take their careers to the next level.

Besides sharing your story and spreading your message, the book you write begins building your legacy beyond the work-place. Think of it as your business card on steroids. Rather than offering merely your name and title, it contains your phi-losophy, your approach, your story, and your identity. A pub-lished book can be the stepping-stone for a speaking, coaching, or consulting career. It builds your brand by positioning you as an international authority in your field. It can help you attract the clients you want and scale your business.

With all this in mind, I've offered a second bonus chapter in *The Guided Author*. It's called 'The Blueprint for Dominating Your Market: From Niche Author to Global Thought Leader'.

This journey is one of growth, not just as an author and commu-nicator, but also as an entrepreneur and thought leader. When I started out on the speaking circuit in Dubai, I literally begged to be on stage, for free! I would take any opportunity to broad-cast my message. But once I'd published my bestselling book, *Live Passionately!*, the bookers started coming to me. I was able to start charging, and charging well. That book made me the go-to speaker on the subject of passion and entrepreneurship.

Writing *Live Passionately!* didn't just open a lot of doors for me. It helped clarify who I wanted to be and what I wanted to do with my career. I never would have become the succssful publisher and executive coach helping others find their voice if I had not found the formula for writing my first book.

So, if your *Why* is about spreading your knowledge and passion, then you've got to write your book. If it's also about advancing your career and getting your name out there, then that's even better. But once the book is done, once you've unwrapped that first copy and celebrated a job well done, don't be surprised if your *Why* — your purpose — changes. Because the book-writing journey is also one of self-discovery. The achievement will change you just as it changed me. The thought and effort you put into the process may well make you see your field, your career, and your life entirely differently.

The Guided Author has been created to reflect the values I have found most important since I began my own author and pub-lisher journeys.

- PASSION: Love what you do and give it your all.
- KEEP IT SIMPLE: Simplify the process, communicate clearly, and be as efficient as you can.
- EVOLVE: Learn from your interactions and grow both as a person and as a leader.
- RESULTS: Deliver what you promise on-time and on-quality.
- ENJOY THE JOURNEY: Celebrate the small wins and have fun along the way. After all, how often do you get to become an author for the first time?

My own mentor, Dr. Marshall Goldsmith, the world's number one executive coach, told me that successful leaders have three things in common: courage, humility, and discipline. You need the courage to own up to everything you are doing. You need the humility to ask for help when you need it. And you need the discipline to deliver on your promises and goals with no excuses. By buying this book, you have demonstrated both courage and humility. *The Guided Author* will give you the help you need to write your book. All that remains is the discipline to follow through with the steps you'll find here. In a month or two, your book will be ready for publishing, and you'll begin making your impact on the world. That's something to celebrate!

You have a message to share.
The world is waiting for your book.

Moustafa Hamwi
The Passionpreneur

CHAPTER

1

I LOVE YOU,
THEN I HATE YOU!

*How the Love-Hate Relationship with Reading
Created One of the World's Leading
Book-Creation Systems*

CHAPTER 1

I LOVE YOU,
THEN I HATE YOU!

How the Love-Hate Relationship with
Reading Created One of the World's Leading
Book-Creation Systems

*"OPPORTUNITY IS MISSED BY MOST PEOPLE
BECAUSE IT IS DRESSED IN OVERALLS AND
LOOKS LIKE WORK."*

— THOMAS EDISON

I HATE WRITING!

Yes, I hate writing. I love teaching and sharing knowledge, but I was never good at writing. My love for sharing knowledge made me figure out a way to write and publish several books of my own, which then led me to become one of the leading publishers of transformational books. More than anything, this journey of mine has been rooted in my own personal transformation, which started when I bought a one-way ticket to India and quit the life of glitz and glamour I was living in Dubai. You can read a longer version of my story in my previous book *Live Passionately*, but to add a little context to this book, I must invite you to step into my world — or at least part of it.

I was the co-founder of a communications firm involved in events, entertainment, and modelling, with 45 full-time employees, a 6,000-square-foot office, and partners who were pretty much ruling the nightlife in town. Our holding group had created the most successful nightlife ventures in Dubai, one of which was a world first: a $30 million restaurant-lounge club designed by the world-renowned fashion designer, Roberto Cavalli.

I will leave it to you to imagine what my lifestyle was like!

Although my life looked super-successful on the outside, like something you'd see in movies and rap videos, I felt completely empty on the inside. Sure enough, I had a nervous breakdown and started waking up every day, dreading going to work — the same job that was once my dream come true!

My business was great, and my lifestyle was enviable, but I wanted more out of life than this golden cage. I kept asking myself, "WHAT AM I DOING WITH MY LIFE?" It became increasingly apparent that having clarity about your passion and purpose affects a lot more than just the direction you take; it impacts your quality of life as it increases the probability of success!

That question, "What am I doing with my life?" triggered me to start an inner search for true passion, purpose, and meaning. That search eventually led me in 2012 to a one-way ticket to India. I had no clear plan about where I would go in the country or even what I would do there. I recall my mother asking me, "What are you going to do in India?" And, without hesitation, I answered, "I'm going to get lost." That's all I knew at that moment.

During my trip, I had what would be best described as a coincidental meeting with Swami Yogananda. He had just stepped out of 13 years of solitude and meditation in a cave and had started teaching wisdom-seekers in his *ashram* in the small village of Vashisht outside the town of Manali in the Himalayas.

I had many deep conversations with him, trying to get an answer about life and the purpose and meaning of everything. During one of them, playing with his long beard, he said to me, "Do you know what you are thirsty for? If you do not know what you are thirsty for, you cannot quench your thirst."

His words made me realise that while I had bought this one-way ticket to India seeking answers, I had not even equipped myself with the most essential element: the right question!

I continued my journey across India and reflected on that question. When I came back to Dubai in 2013, I delivered a TEDx-style inspirational talk about my journey. A few months later, something completely unexpected happened. A total stranger walked up to me in the street one day and said, "Are you that speaker guy? You changed my life!" That was a moment I will never forget. I had a feeling that you have also surely felt; that moment when you know you can make a positive impact and be of service to the world.

The more people told me, "You changed my life," the more my inner voice told me, "You should write a book." The problem was that I lacked good writing skills. If anything, I actually hated writing! So, I decided to get into public speaking.

I managed to launch myself as a speaker, sharing the story of my India journey. I began by doing MC work to open up for A-list speakers. Basically, I took on such gigs for free, in exchange for five minutes of my own stage time. By the time I got going, though, the speaking market was already getting overcrowded. I needed a way to differentiate myself from the rest of the speakers out there. The thought of putting a book out crossed my mind, but it seemed like too big a step.

So, I parked the idea of writing a book and did what most speakers were doing at that time — I launched a talk show around my speciality topic: Passion. Two years later, I had conducted in excess of 160 in-person interviews with the world's top people in every field: leaders, executives, sports champions and experts. One of the most memorable and amazing of those interviews was with Dr Marshall Goldsmith (the world's #1 executive coach and a three-time NYT bestselling author).

Dr Goldsmith went on to become a dear friend and mentor, and his guidance had a huge impact on my speaking and coaching career. I talked to him about how challenging it was to maintain my position as the expert on my topic in such an overcrowded digital world, where anyone with a mobile phone can simply post online content. His simple advice was, "Write a book." He also gave me some insights into how he wrote his own books.

It seemed clear that becoming an internationally recognised author was the next step for any successful thought leader. There was no escaping it. But I did not have the skills to produce a decent blog post, let alone a book.

THE GHOST TOOK MY MONEY!

As time passed, the urge to write a book increased in me, so I decided to do what most of us do when seeking answers — I Googled the process. The advice that came up most often was: "Try to write a little every day." So, I began to wake up at 5 am every day and tried to write, but it just didn't work for me. After trying to get down my thoughts for days, all I ended up with was a few scattered notes that, I can safely say now, would not even have amounted to a coherent chapter.

I simply did not know where to begin, how to structure things, how much to write in each section, how to develop ideas. I was lost. A few months into my failed writing experiment, I realised that most of the advice on the internet was geared towards writing fiction, novels or screenplays, which were all very far from what I was trying to create — an inspirational book.

I still had no idea how to get through the writing process, but I was determined to make the book happen. Eventually, I came up with plan B — hiring a ghost-writer.

Yes, hiring someone else to write the book was a much more expensive route, but if that was the only way I could get my book out, then so be it. I was confident that my content was great, and I was so committed to making this book happen that I sold my beloved Harley-Davidson to finance the venture. I was determined to achieve my goal, and nothing was going to stop me!

So, I spent time searching, shortlisting and interviewing ghost-writers until I found the one who seemed to be a perfect fit — a professional ghost-writer living isolated in the countryside and taking up projects remotely. This was someone who could completely focus and stay dedicated to writing the book for me. I had finally found the solution to my struggles; selling my bike would not be in vain! I took a week off work so I could focus 24/7 on the writing journey with my ghost-writer and ... to cut a long story short, it was simply a disaster.

I learned the hard way that no one can sound like you: *only you can sound like you!* What my ghost-writer had written was very well-structured. It was grammatical, even well-written, but it lacked the soul of what I was trying to say and how I would say it. It was more like a news bulletin from the BBC than something to inspire others. Remember, no matter how well the English is structured, people do not get inspired by just the facts; they want to feel the sincerity of the story and the authenticity in the tone of the teacher. People want to hear about real experiences, not made-up versions.

So here I was, a couple of years down the line, thousands of dollars poorer and many of hours wasted. I had failed to write the book in any way, shape or form. But my drive to teach and share was not fading, so I put the idea of writing a book on the back burner and resorted to what I do well naturally: speaking.

I distilled the knowledge I had gained from all these interviews into an in-person workshop that I tested on hundreds of people in different countries. As I developed the content, I was also getting a lot of mentorship from some of the world's best coaches, many of whom I was interviewing. The final outcome was a multi-disciplinary workshop that incorporated all the learning I had gained from the knowledge experts had shared during the interviews, and from the techniques they had shown me.

One method that proved very useful was the late Professor Tony Buzan's mind-mapping techniques. They gave me insight into the blueprinting process that I would go on to use in my online courses and, eventually, in the writing system I will be sharing with you in this book.

Being a perfectionist, however, I was still not confident about considering myself as fit to teach others. So, I took a step back from most of my day-to-day work to focus on creating the best teaching strategies as well as the best structure and content for the course. I was determined to create something that had an impact and brought results.

After more than a year of testing the workshop with focus groups and running it in different countries, I felt that I had created an inspiring online course. It was an amazing success, but that success was not enough to push the idea of a book out of my head; especially after almost every leading expert, coach or speaker I interviewed said the same thing to me: "Write a book."

I came to terms with the fact that there is a glass ceiling, one I would not break through until I became an author. Once again, I found myself stuck in a tug-of-war between my love for learning and sharing and my lack of affection for reading and writing. Audio books and online courses saved the day when it came to my own learning; conducting workshops helped me with the sharing. But none of that could scratch the itch, that elusive dream of becoming an author.

LESSONS FROM READING 30,000 BOOKS

During a conversation with one of my mentors, Dr John Demartini, I had a light-bulb moment, one that I had been awaiting for a long time.

Before I share what he said to me, I should tell you that Dr Demartini is known for his speed-reading technique, which enabled him to study over 30,000 books across all the defined academic disciplines. He is also the author of 40 books published in 29 different languages, has created over 72 different courses and produced over 60 CDs and DVDs.

I was not a good teacher yet, but I was a great student. When such world-class mentors give advice, I listen carefully and follow through. And what he told me that day was that many of his books were produced by getting someone to record and transcribe his conversations.

Aha! So, "getting help" with writing does not necessarily mean getting a ghost-writer. That was a revelation for me. Having that moment of recognition made me realise that I'd actually had the advice before, back when Dr Marshall Goldsmith was telling me to write a book. He told me that he did not actually write his three books alone but had had help with them. Not long after that, he specifically said what that help was: he recorded his thoughts, and someone else transcribed them for him.

I guess I didn't really absorb the advice until I was ready for it. Maybe I had been a little intimidated: after all, Dr Demartini and Dr Goldsmith were both highly educated and well-recognised, and I was not *Dr* Moustafa Hamwi. Could I really follow their method to create a new book? Could it really be that easy? But they and other mentors assured me that the method was sound. It seemed that only a few hours of recording were needed; this was very different from the many, many hours I thought a book would require.

Well, I already had hours of filmed content for my online course, which was built on a solid structure after a lot of research and testing. So, I simply gathered the content I already had — which I knew was what I wanted my book to be about — and got it all transcribed. Once I had the transcription in hand, it served me as the first draft of my book. I then edited the content and structured it into chapters in the way I wanted, and reverse-engineered everything I had into a book.

The amazing thing was that, since the content of my course was originally designed to coach and guide rather than lecture, the book that emerged had the same practical approach. It was more engaging, enjoyable and impactful than a traditionally written book would have been.

LET'S GET THE PARTY STARTED

Finally, I had done it. My years of struggle were over, and I had developed a new approach to producing books. No more typing and spending hours trying to put the content together. All that was needed was about four hours of recording to create a book, one that might run up to two hundred pages.

Since then, creating books has become a systematic process for me. It requires true passion for the topic I am talking about, some blueprinting (you'll read more about that in coming chapters), some short recording sessions, and boom... I create a book! So now I have evolved from being a wannabe author struggling to even write a chapter, to producing a book a year.

At the time of writing this book, I have already co-authored a book with Brian Tracy, and published 3 international best-sellers of my own, and produced this book — and I have a couple more in the making. Remember, I am a person who is not fond of reading and struggles with writing even a decent blog post.

The personal brand I've built on the back of being a bestselling author has taken me from struggling to get on stage — even for free — to getting paid in excess of $10,000 per talk and attracting the kind of clients I like to work with. More importantly, it has enabled me to build several businesses around my brand name and launch them digitally, allowing me the freedom of living anywhere in the world and not just staying tied to a desk.

This proved to be most valuable when the COVID pandemic struck. While most businesses were struggling, my businesses were growing, and I owe a big part of that to becoming an international author. Still, nothing has come close to getting a "you changed my life" message from one of my readers, and that gave me the drive to expand that impact even further, beyond just me.

One thing I learned from my previous businesses in nightlife is that you cannot have a party on your own; so why not create a global passion party?!

This drive to spread passion and purposeful living in the world, by enabling inspiring leaders like you to share their stories and have a positive impact, is what gives me the ultimate fulfilment. This is what I call a "joyful mission". It's about creating the conditions that enable us to share the fruits of a more passionate and purposeful world. Enabling more people to serve means that I'm serving too. I'm simply getting an energetic commission on the whole deal.

That's why I was driven to launch Passionpreneur Publishing, where we have helped (to date) in excess of 100 high-performing leaders like you (none of whom are professional writers) become international authors in just a matter of months. I have worked with them to bring their knowledge out of their heads and into bestselling books that help change people's lives — and, of course, their own.

Throughout this book I will share with you relevant snippets from the success stories of our authors; however, if you would like to get a full scoop of such stories, you can read them at www.PassionpreneurPublishing.com/success-stories.

But more important than our past success stories is the question I want to ask you: "WHAT WILL YOUR OWN AUTHOR SUCCESS STORY BE?"

FROM AN IDEA TO A CLOCKWORK SYSTEM

Of course, having passion and purpose was a great start, but replicating my own success with other aspiring authors, in a systematic manner, was a different ballgame altogether. After all, being a great football player and being a coach who develops great football players are two totally different things.

At the end of the day, I am not a writing specialist. How would I be able to create a tribe of authors?

To be clear, I did not invent the concept of recording and transcribing. The idea has existed for quite a while and is used by many book coaches out there, some of whom we worked with at the early stage of our business. The problem was that none of them had developed an end-to-end system. Most of these coaches and writing specialists do not have solid corporate careers or credible executive coaching experience. Their approaches utilise old-school writing methodologies mixed with ad-hoc gimmicks to make their solutions more exciting.

Such dated solutions are more a matter of trial and error than a consistent, successful process. I saw that following them would be a waste of precious time and energy, and I know that successful leaders like you have enough on their plate already.

My way of doing things then was just as it is now, "Do it with passion or not at all." If we were going to disrupt the way transformational books are created, I had to play a different game. My focus was simple and direct: "How to create an end-to-end system to get the best output without enormous input?" I wanted to use this system to benefit people like me, people who have a passion to share but have limited writing skills and very little time to spare.

So, I tapped into years of professional experience in different disciplines, utilised my access to the world's best mentors and coaches, solicited the help of highly experienced book coaches, editors and traditional publishers, and invested a couple of years into synthesizing all this learning to create the *Guided Author System*. I put the right strategies, methodologies and processes together into a structured system. And it was only once we succeeded with helping 100 authors through this system that we decided to publish it in this book.

To give you some insight into the range of knowledge that I and my team invested into the Guided Author System, let me share with you what all of it incorporated — everything ranging from scientific knowledge about structuring your thoughts; PR and communication disciplines; the drama structure used in storytelling and movies; study and analysis of the world's top speakers, coaches and authors; executive coaching techniques;

and dozens of relevant certifications in the fields of NLP, Hypnotherapy, Meditation and others.

KEEPING IT SIMPLE

In short, there are a few cornerstones to the system we have developed:

- Be strategic: know your niche and the big WHY behind writing the book
- Follow a proven roadmap: utilise best-practice systems to guide your efforts to write a book that delivers on its promise
- Do it efficiently: you only do the important parts, the parts that only you can do, the top-level thinking. Everything else you outsource.

In the coming chapters, I will dive deeper into the science behind this system, and more importantly, how it can be used to help inspiring and passionate thought leaders like you share your message with the world and become *global* thought leaders, in the most efficient way possible.

But before all of that, you want to make sure that you are, and stay, motivated to write your book. This first condition requires you to be crystal-clear about the big WHY behind writing your book, which is what we will be discussing in the next chapter.

CHAPTER

2

DO NOT WRITE A BOOK UNLESS YOU ARE FOR REAL

Why and How to Finally Do It

DO NOT WRITE A BOOK UNLESS YOU ARE FOR REAL

Why and How to Finally Do It

"THERE COMES A POINT IN YOUR LIFE WHEN YOU NEED TO STOP READING OTHER PEOPLE'S BOOKS AND WRITE YOUR OWN."

– ALBERT EINSTEIN

YOU HAVE A MESSAGE TO SHARE

Do you feel you have a message to share, a story to tell, or a lesson to teach?

If so, you should think about writing a book.

I know what you are thinking. "Really? Just because I want to share something good with the world, I should be writing a book? How about a blog post instead?"

Yes, the idea of writing a blog may seem attractive, but there is nothing that will ever compare to becoming an international author. And there is simply nothing like the feeling you get when you hold your book in your hands. Like I said previously, it's kind of like having a baby. Once you step into parenthood, life is never the same.

So, in this chapter, I will be talking about:

- The number one reason to become an author (and no, it's not about book sales)
- Other reasons why you should write a book
- How to get yourself moving so you can finally achieve your dream.

Are you ready to go on this journey with me?

REALITY CHECK

I know that most of us who embark on the journey of writing a book dream about hitting the bestseller list or making big sales in bookstores or online selling platforms. But before we delve deeper into these topics, here's a quick reality check for you.

Most people don't make a lot of money with their book sales on Amazon. Chances are that you will not be in the one percent of people who actually do, at least not in the early stages of your writing career. But don't despair. The more important thing you need to know is that there are more profitable ways to improve the return on investment (ROI) of your book.

According to a recent study by the Authors Guild,[1] the income of full-time authors dropped by 30% between 2009 and 2015 (and this was before COVID came along). Let me crunch the numbers for you. The traditional publishing model works on paying you 3-5% of book sales. Assuming your book sells at $20 and you are getting the best deal (5%), you will be left with only $1 per book sold. Even if you are content with living off $2,000 per month, you need to sell at least 24,000 books annually, just so you have the same standard of living you had when you were in your early twenties.

So, it's safe to say that book sales should NOT be your primary motivation for writing a book.

THEN WHY SHOULD YOU EVEN BOTHER WRITING A BOOK?

There are many reasons why you should be writing a book, and yes, having a profit margin is definitely one of them — and there are ways in which you can get a tenfold return on your investment. So, what is the most important reason to write a book?

---

1   https://www.authorsguild.org/the-writing-life/why-is-it-so-goddamned-hard-to-make-a-living-as-a-writer-today/

Building Authority

Let's face it, who doesn't want to be the go-to authority in their field?

As I have said, do it with passion or don't do it at all. If you are not really bringing your A-game, why are you doing what you do? Think about it: how many people in your field have published valuable books?

Mohanad Alwadiya, dubbed the Wolf of Real Estate in Dubai, had a few million followers on social media. After he published his book, people started referring to him at that time as *"the author of the only book on real estate investing in the UAE"*. This happened to such an extent that the content of his book became the certification manual for real estate professionals.

In telling his author success story, Mohanad said this: "I remember Moustafa saying, 'Being an author will bring you authority'. I am so fortunate that I am experiencing that now. Being an international author has brought me more credibility and cemented my experience and reputation in the real estate industry. In the last two years, we have managed to sell more than 90,000 copies of *Landlording,* something I never dreamt of achieving. That has brought me a lot of exposure and a lot of financial gains. My book has become my business card."

Mohanad was one of the first Passionpreneur Authors, and truly the first proof that the Guided Author System worked.

He already had passion and excellence in his field. He was already driven and ready to level-up. But becoming an author gave him another level of recognition and credibility. These days, the book goes with him everywhere. It is more than a business card. It is the foundation and essence of who he is as an entrepreneur, an authority, and a thought leader and it is right there in tangible form.

Google recognises this level of authority in a way money cannot buy, and no amount of search engine optimisation (SEO) can imitate that. Did you know that, according to the SEO Journal,[2] Amazon is the world's third-largest search engine after Google and YouTube, and way ahead of Facebook and Bing?

Many of our authors had almost no positioning on Google before they published their books. If you typed their name into Google, lots of people with similar names appeared. But now, after having their book published, you will probably find them dominating the first page on Google, often with a knowledge panel on the right — a feature reserved for authority figures, and one that money cannot buy.

So, it's safe to say that the most important reason for writing a book is this:

---

2   https://www.searchenginejournal.com/seo-101/meet-search-engines/#close

Author = Authority

Now, you might think there are already too many "authorities" in your field of expertise or that your topic is not really new. But the truth is, it does not really matter whether it has been said and done hundreds of times. Your approach towards the topic and the way you communicate your message are new and unique. The way you service your market niche through your book is what will make you stand out from the self-proclaimed authorities.

If anything, this proves that when you have the right level of passion, combined with the right strategy and the support of a professional publisher, you can stand out against the crowd in your market niche.

Furthermore, becoming an author is your entry ticket to a bigger game: becoming a Global Thought Leader. And if you want to play in the Pro League, you need to have Pro Tools.

OTHER KEY REASONS WHY YOU SHOULD WRITE A BOOK

Launching Your Speaking/Coaching/ Consulting Business

Becoming a highly paid speaker is the Holy Grail for people who have an important message to share. If you think about it, all the world's legendary speakers and coaches, such as Tony Robbins and Jack Canfield, have more than one book to their name. Some of them, like Brian Tracy and Dr Marshall Goldsmith, have in excess of 30 books.

One of the best examples I can give is how Dr Corrie Block used his book to skyrocket the growth of his consulting business. In his own words:

"THE BOOK HELPED ME CEMENT MY CREDIBILITY AGAINST WHAT USED TO BE MY COMPETITION UNTIL I PUBLISHED THE BOOK, NOW I AM VIEWED AS THE GO-TO EXPERT WHEN IT COMES TO EXECUTIVE HIGH PERFORMANCE."

Attracting clients you like

If you are looking for a steady flow of quality leads — the kind of clients that energise rather than drain you — a book is the best lead generation tool. Your book can also help to educate clients on your methodologies, which means they become much easier to work with.

I've seen this time after time: the strategy behind the book becomes the guidepost for the content within it. When your book is finally launched, it can attract clients who understand the value of your services. This is why many of our authors are highly sought-after leaders, speakers, coaches and mentors.

Sharing your story and leaving a legacy

Do you have a story that you believe will inspire others, a message to share with the world? Do you want to leave a legacy for future generations?

If your answer is yes, then writing a book is the best way to do that. And it's not just about you; that legacy might be from loved ones who are not with us anymore. Let me tell you the story of Noreen Nasralla, a woman who wanted to honour the memory of her father, Abdin Nasralla, a hospitality legend in Dubai. After his passing, she collected the notes he had left about how to excel in the hospitality industry. We helped her publish *Passionate Hoteliers*, which became an Amazon #1 bestseller. What better way to honour the memory of her father?

Sharing your story can be a great tool for healing the world, and yourself in the process. A great example I can give is of that of Abbood Tamimi, who had a unique and haunting life story. His journey had taken him to rock bottom following severe childhood trauma, but Abbood had the courage to form this into life-changing wisdom on how to recover from trauma and forge a way ahead into entrepreneurship. Through our strategy sessions, Abbood had the courage to open up about the trauma of suffering from child abuse and the gruelling work of recovery. Publishing his book was a major part of his healing, and more importantly it helped others realise they are not alone. They can speak up about what happened and use his book as a tool to heal their soul and turn their trauma into fuel that helps them launch their entrepreneurial venture — something Abbood calls being a Soulpreneur.

In short, whichever way you look at it, books get attention and attention gives you the power to grow your business and increase your impact.

A BIG KICK IN THE BUT!

No matter how motivated you are, sometimes there is a barrier (the big 'but') that stops you from achieving your dreams. So, if you feel that something is holding you back, don't worry, because I have a two-step approach you can follow:

A. Understand the barriers that have been holding you back from achieving your dream of becoming an international author and the authority you deserve to be.
B. Learn the best ways to overcome them.

Let's start with understanding the obstacles that have been holding you back from becoming an international author.

To date, my team and I have worked with over 100 authors, which means we have looked at 500–1,000 potential authors to see if they would be a good fit for our publishing program. In the process, we have realised that the majority of the ones who do not manage to start their journey, or start but never finish, have very similar reasons for why they couldn't make it. Here are the top five reasons why people never finish their books:

 1. Do not have time: This seems to be the #1 reason why people put off their dream of writing and publishing a book. They are too overloaded with work or family responsibilities and have hardly any time for themselves.

 2. Do not have the money: There are a lot of people who might really want to write and publish a book, but they don't know how to come up with the money required to make it happen.

 3. Confused about the writing and publishing process: This is something a lot of people who come to us share. Most aspiring writers are not familiar with all the activities involved in writing a book and bringing it to market.

 4. Not sure they have the right content: Many people are not convinced that they have the right content, or the right topic, for their project. In a nutshell, they may not be confident about their idea for a book.

 5. Will do it tomorrow: Procrastination is something many people struggle with, and aspiring authors are no exception. They tend to keep putting off their book until the time is right (and somehow, really, the time is *never* right).

Do any of the above sound familiar to you? You may feel that more than one apply to you.

And you know what?

All of these are valid excuses.

Yes, you read that right. We can't say that they're not valid. But they are — and will remain — *excuses.*

So, if you are serious about becoming an international author, here is a list of our bulletproof strategies to help you overcome the barriers and achieve your dream of publishing your book.

 1. Time

If you are saying you are overloaded and do not have time, the solution is to focus. Understand that everybody has 24 hours — and only 24 hours — in any given day. Whether you are a president, an employee, a sports personality, or a business owner, 24 hours is what you get, each and every day.

This includes all the authors we have worked with, and they managed to write and publish their books — married or single, having children or not, it doesn't really matter. We have authors with three or more children who are doing a day job and building their business in the evenings, but they still manage to find time to write. We also know people who are single, who gave up on their books or never started their journey.

If you are unable to carve the hours required to bring your dream to reality into your schedule, then how can you hope to achieve anything in life? The reality is, if something is truly meaningful to you, you *will* find the time for it. If you have children, you will know what I mean. Before you had them, you thought there was not enough time in your day. But once the children came into your life, suddenly you had to find ways to create time to take care of them.

It's just a question of priorities.

 **2. Money**

If the story you tell yourself is that you do not have the money right now, we will tell you one thing: Successful entrepreneurs think, "How can I get a return on investment?"

Do not think of it as an expense. Don't look at it as money spent that is never coming back. If you think of it as an *investment*, the question you want to answer is, "How can I get a return on my investment?" Then it becomes a business decision.

If I told you today that you can buy a house for a small down-payment and an instalment plan, and that this house's worth is going to double, triple, or quadruple in a year, would you be willing to use your credit card, or find some other way to buy the house? Or would you rather get the same loan or use the same credit card to buy something that depreciates — like a car, a suite of furniture or a piece of jewellery?

If you are buying something as an investment, then you will work on growing it. But if you buy things that depreciate, you will end up being more broke than when you started.

There is no better example of this than one of the authors we mentioned earlier, Mohanad Alwadiya, the author of *Landlording*. His book became the #1 book in real estate investments in the region, and more importantly, the book generated leads for him, which converted into real estate deals worth millions of dollars.

*"SUCCESSFUL ENTREPRENEURS THINK ABOUT
ROI, NOT EXPENSES."*

 ### 3. Confused about the writing and publishing process

This book you are reading is the solution to this problem. I will guide you through the most efficient way to create your book, with the least effort on your part.

 ### 4. Not sure if you have the right content

My only answer to that is:

You never will – until you believe in yourself.

How many years have you been a professional? Five years? Ten years? Do you believe you can share one or two lessons you have learned from each year of your professional life? Can you talk about each of those for just twenty minutes? That's all you need to produce the book that you have always wanted to write.

How old do you have to be before you are confident that you have the right content to share? Will you wait until you are in your eighties or nineties? Are you sure you are still going to be on the planet then?

Remember: it's not only about how much knowledge you have, it's about how much passion you have.

Last, but not least, the most common excuse is:

 ## 5. I Will Do it Tomorrow

The biggest excuse we all have is, "I will do it tomorrow".

Let me ask you, how long have you been saying "tomorrow"? How many dreams are going to die while you're still saying tomorrow? My friend, it's now or never; tomorrow never comes.

Your dream is never going to happen if you don't take action. Now.

Of the hundreds of people I did a pre-qualifying call to help them publish a book they are thinking of, anybody who said, "I will get back to you," never finished their book. Those who took action immediately achieved their dream. They started their journey with me and my team, and finished it, even if it took them some time.

The most inspiring example of someone who adopted this "no-excuses" mentality to achieve her dream of becoming an international author is Pegah Gol. She came to me wanting to write and publish a book. Right at the onset, she had more challenges than most of the people I have worked with. She did not even have a job to finance the book-writing journey, but she still signed up with us and said, "Give me some time. I'm going to arrange the money."

She went ahead and managed to get herself a job. Soon after she got started writing, she got struck with another tragedy, the death of her beloved mother. She was held back, but she didn't give up. She still found time in her schedule, despite all the obstacles. She fell behind on the publishing schedule, but she kept writing.

Pegah wasn't sure about the money, so she got a job. She was confused about the writing and publishing process and was even unsure about her content. She used our help and let us guide and support her throughout the whole process ... and guess what?

She ended up writing a book about how to find your dream job, *The Formula*. The book became an Amazon #1 bestseller within 24 hours of its launch. After that, she quit her job and began her own business, helping people write the best CVs, and hunt for their dream job.

Pegah did not say, "I'll do it tomorrow." She took the first step and kept going.

INTERESTED IN WRITING A BOOK?
GO TO THE MOVIES

If you are interested but not necessarily passionate about writing your book, then go to the movies. At a movie, you just sit and watch life go by on the screen. It's only when you are genuinely committed, not just interested, that you can achieve your goals, dreams and aspirations.

But… is it going to be easy?

We do our best to make it as simple as possible with the *Guided Author* methodology.

But… is it going to be worth it?

You tell me. Are you willing to do what it takes to become a recognised authority in your field and stand out from the rest of the crowd?

If your answer to both questions is yes, then say, "I am committed" right out loud and turn to the next chapter, where I will introduce you to the Guided Author System.

So, only if you are "serious and committed," proceed to the next section.

You Have a Message to Share.
The World is Waiting for Your Book.

3

THE SIMPLEST WAY TO DO THE HARDEST THING

The Guided Author System

CHAPTER 3

THE SIMPLEST WAY TO DO THE HARDEST THING

The Guided Author System

"EVERYTHING MUST BE MADE AS SIMPLE AS POSSIBLE. BUT NOT SIMPLER."

– ALBERT EINSTEIN

WELCOME TO THE GUIDED AUTHOR JOURNEY

I'm thrilled that you have committed to becoming an international author and sharing your message with the world, and that you chose the right passion tribe to help you on this journey.

It is my mission to help inspiring leaders like you share your message with the world and become Global Thought Leaders, so we can, collectively, spread passion and purpose in the world.

Our aim in the Guided Author journey is to get you to experience the same level of success that I — and many of our authors — have experienced.

In this chapter, I will share more about the science behind the Guided Author System, and the key stages of the writing journey.

WHY DO YOU NEED A SYSTEM? CAN'T YOU JUST WING IT?

The fact that you are reading this book means one of two things: You have attempted to create your book but have not made much progress; or you are the kind of person that needs a clear roadmap before you embark on a new venture.

In both cases, the Guided Author System is the perfect solution for you because it:

- **Keeps things simple:** We have broken down the whole writing and publishing journey into easy-to-handle chunks to make the process as efficient as possible. Simple means you will stay on top of things, avoid being overwhelmed and get the book finished.
- **Provides a clear roadmap:** When you have such a clear roadmap, it becomes easier to manage your time and energy, the two most valuable resources of a successful leader. Clarity means certainty, certainty breeds focus, and focus breeds results.

WHAT IS SO SPECIAL ABOUT THE GUIDED AUTHOR SYSTEM?

In the first chapter, I shared with you the story of how the Guided Author System evolved. Using this system means you are getting a synthesis of best practice in every single area that might be relevant to producing a thought-leadership book. Among them are:

 The science of structuring your thoughts: This includes a variety of techniques, like mind mapping logic, invented by my late mentor, Professor Tony Buzan (who was also a Nobel Prize nominee) and the legendary Brian Tracy's simple logic behind teaching any topic to anyone in a simple manner.

 PR and communication: I started my career handling PR and communications for brands like Nokia, Cisco, and Showtime. If we consider your book as a PR activity, then it offers two lessons: 1) how to develop a message that gets the right attention, and 2) how to use the book *itself* to generate the right publicity.

 Analysing the Dramatic Arc: The dramatic arc is a storytelling technique used in successful movies, plays and novels. It can be studied, understood and applied to your book to make it as appealing as possible to a wide audience.

 Studying and analysing the performance of the world's top speakers, coaches and authors: When I investigated the world's top speakers, I observed common patterns in their communication style (both written and spoken) that can be incorporated into your book to create the most impact.

Studying the highest converting platform-selling professional: Platform-selling professionals are speakers who make their money by selling from the stage, instead of charging a speaking fee. The top skill these speakers possess is the ability to get the audience to say "yes" and pay money for their services. This skill is vital if you want to convert your book readers into clients.

 My experience as an international speaker: Charging in excess of $10,000 for an hour on stage, and also being a platform-selling speaker with one of the highest conversion rates in the industry, I have gleaned a lot of insight into the kind of language to use to get emotional engagement from the audience.

 Executive-coaching skills: We utilise one of the best-known executive-coaching systems, created by Dr Marshall Goldsmith, the world's #1 executive and leadership coach.

In addition to all this, I have taken dozens of relevant certifications in the fields of NLP, Hypnotherapy, Meditation and much more and synthesised these disciplines into a structured and systematic approach.

DOES THIS WORK FOR EVERYBODY?

No, it does not.

I have already talked about having interest vs having commitment. I learned from Dr Marshall Goldsmith that we can only help leaders to become more successful if they demonstrate three criteria: Courage, Humility and Discipline.

 Courage, to face your fears

 Humility, to ask for help when you need it

 Discipline, to deliver with no excuses

The Guided Author System is designed specifically to cater to leaders, entrepreneurs, executives and high-performing experts. You do not need to be a writer, but you do need to be an expert in your field; and you need to have passion for the topic and the mission of becoming a global thought leader. If you have all these qualities, the book becomes just another step towards that big dream.

One of my highlights was working with Anthony Joseph. He finished creating his book content in a month, right before his wedding. Anthony was not a writer nor an academic. He came from humble beginnings and began to make an impact in real estate, then he wanted to go to the next level, becoming an authority in his field.

Strategy and blueprinting were the keys to him achieving this with such speed and effectiveness. He followed the system step by step from the strategy session to blueprinting with one of our book coaches. From there, he used his phone to record each chapter and finished his content creation in just one month.

The Guided Author system helped him stay focused and efficient. Anthony went on his honeymoon while the publishing team worked their magic, and when he came back it was ready to go. Not only that, it quickly hit Amazon #1 bestseller and Anthony is now reaping the benefits in terms of market positioning and global recognition.

Would he have been able to achieve this if he hadn't partnered with someone who could help bring simplicity to a process that can be so overwhelming? Would he be able to write a book at all, being that putting pen to paper wasn't his strong point? Who knows? But I suspect not.

The Guided Author System helped Christian develop a laser focus, and an engaging writing style. In fact, he brought his Italian heritage into it in creating "The Pizza Guide for Digital Marketing." No longer was this immense topic too big to fit into one book. It was focused, engaging, and actionable, and even made the Amazon top 50 bestsellers list in its class. He continues to see the benefits of becoming an international author as clients find him through his book. But would it have happened if he hadn't have partnered with someone who could help bring simplicity to a process that can be so overwhelming? Who knows? But I suspect not.

The Mantra that is built into Passionpreneur Publishing is that we keep it simple. But this simplicity comes from doing years of analysis and learning so I could distil all of that into a system that our authors could easily follow.

THE GUIDED AUTHOR JOURNEY HAS 7 KEY STAGES

 1. Strategy and Planning

 2. Blueprints

 3. Content Creation

 4. Bells and Whistles

 5. Publishing

 6. Book Cover and Marketing Kit

 7. Home Run – getting ready to launch

You will find a chapter of this book dedicated to each of these key stages. In addition, I have included a couple of bonus chapters for you to enjoy and profit from:

LET THE WORLD KNOW – *How to Plan an Effective Book Launch*

 THE BLUEPRINT FOR DOMINATING YOUR MARKET NICHE – *From Author to Global Thought Leader*

Now, let's elaborate a little bit on the stages of the Guided Author System. Again, I will dive deeper into each one in the coming chapters.

 ### 1. Strategy and Planning

This is the first and most important part of your writing journey. Strategy is key to achieving success in any endeavour you take up, and book writing is no exception. Without proper planning and strategy, your book will never get off the launch pad.

In this stage of the journey, you will find your ideal niche, target audience, and the key messages you want to deliver. This stage also involves the overall book-project planning, including a celebration plan, which will work as a motivating factor for you to sail through the whole journey.

 ### 2. Blueprints

Imagine trying to build a tower without having proper architectural drawings and engineering plans... well, you also need what we call "blueprints" to build your book. They're the skeleton that will carry the rest of the body around it. Without blueprints, your thoughts will remain scattered, and you won't be able to build your book. Even worse, you might create something that backfires on you by having a confused or incomplete message.

3. Content Creation

This is where you put the meat on the bones. Once you have taken the first two steps, content creation is about filling in the blanks, either through our unique recording methodology, or typing if you prefer.

4. Bells and Whistles

Would you prefer your car to be stripped down and basic or top of the range? It might not change the duration of the trip, but it will surely change the experience — both during the journey and when you show up at your destination.

The simplest way to think of the "bells and whistles" of your book is to see them as the icing on the cake. You want to include testimonials, acknowledgements, calls to action and specific guidance for the reader to take the next step with you — among other elements that will make your book as impressive as possible. From experience, I can say that icing makes the cake taste a lot better.

5. Publishing

This is the stage where your work becomes more about review and approval, and the hard part is left to the publishers. This stage involves the editing, typesetting and design of your book.

6. Book Cover and Marketing Kit

While a book cover is always an important part of the publishing journey, we see it as absolutely crucial. To us, your book is your business card on steroids. It is not the end product; it is your introduction as the global expert in your area. You really want it to make an impression. That is why I have dedicated an entire chapter to the different skills that go into creating an impressive cover, starting with the photoshoot and writing the cover brief, and including all other marketing elements impacted by your cover.

7. Home Run

At this point, you are just a few steps away from officially becoming an international author. There remains to be a few things to get in order like pricing your book, setting up your global distribution and printing your book.

Beyond publishing, the below two steps are covered in the bonus chapters

LET THE WORLD KNOW – *How to Plan an Effective Book Launch*

Once all the tasks involved in publishing your book are complete, it's time to let the world know about you and your book.

The great news about this is that it is a lot easier than you think. In this bonus chapter, I will show you how to conduct the most efficient book launch, one that reaches your target audience and gets you the results you want. I will also discuss how to choose the most suitable launch date, the must-do elements of your launch and the best ways to get the most out of your launch efforts.

 FROM AUTHOR TO THOUGHT LEADER: *The Blueprint for Dominating Your Market Niche*
One of the most common questions I am asked is, "Okay, I've just finished my book, what happens next?"

For most publishers, the goal is to publish the book, but we see it as the beginning of your journey towards becoming a Global Thought Leader. So, in this bonus chapter, I will share some insights gained from the coaching I do with our authors on how to get the best return on investment and how to use your book to position yourself as the authority in your field.

IT'S THAT SIMPLE

Writing a book is not as difficult a task as a lot of people think it is. When you have the necessary passion and a clear commitment to making it to the shelves, and you come up with a clear-cut plan, the whole writing journey becomes a cakewalk.

Oh, and one more thing: *Enjoy the journey! Celebrate the small wins and have fun along the way.* After all, how often do you get to become an author for the first time? To help keep this journey a fun one, we will remind you to celebrate at the end of each chapter when you finish your tasks, starting with this one!

Please note all worksheets mentioned in this book along with bonuses and other valuable assets to help you on your thought leadership journey are available for you to download for free on this page https:// PassionpreneurPublishing.com/free-book-resources

**For now, well done!
Time to reward yourself.**

CHAPTER

4

FIND YOUR NICHE

Defining Your Big Why and
Planning the Journey

FIND YOUR NICHE

Defining Your Big Why and
Planning the Journey

*"SUCCESS IS 20% SKILLS AND
80% STRATEGY AND PLANNING."*

— JIM ROHN

BEGIN WITH THE END IN MIND

Content is the star of the book. After all, your content is your message. But if you do not know your ultimate goal for writing the book and the key audience you want to serve, then you won't know how to formulate that message in a way to bring you ROI on all fronts (impact, money and brand). This is something I learned from my career in communications and public relations. Know your audience and know your message. When you do, it will be easy to speak to them in a way that resonates and has impact. Otherwise, you'll pour your heart into the book, but the message will not be received by the reader.

To achieve these goals, we use a strategy blueprint. This document is the cornerstone of your personal brand, not just your book. So make sure you invest the right level of energy into this process as it will shape your trajectory on your journey into authorhood and thought-leadership.

By the end of this chapter, you will be able to identify your ideal market niche, develop a laser-focused elevator pitch, create a book that delivers on its promise, outline the relevant key messages in each chapter, and then put a project plan together. In other words, you will be able to create a clear strategy and roadmap to achieve your goal of becoming an international author.

As a bonus, I am also going to give you a celebration plan template and a "Passion Meditation" to help you see your book as a reality, starting today.

TAKE A STEP BACK BEFORE TAKING TWO STEPS FORWARD

Think about a time when you did something without thinking it through, perhaps as a part of your work, or something that you'd always wanted to do in your life. How well did it work? It was probably stressful, or you might have gotten lucky, but hope is not a strategy. Think how well things can go when you have a strategic approach and a clear plan.

Having a clear idea of what to do makes doing it a thousand times easier. You don't have to follow a trial-and-error method to see what works; and you definitely don't have to repeat the same thing over and over. It saves time and effort, but it will give you much better results. When it comes to writing a book, it is important for you to come up with a fool-proof plan that will help you breeze through the process — and make it a whole lot of fun, too.

Let me give you an example. Hanane Benkhalouk, one of our authors, found the entire writing process easy once she was crystal-clear about her strategy. We went through the strategy together, finding the exact niche that her book would impact and crafting a way forward that would hit the mark. After doing that necessary strategy work, she began writing about how to navigate through a world full of VUCA (Volatility, Uncertainty, Complexity and Ambiguity).

But with the unexpected shock of COVID disrupting our lives at a global level, she had to change course. Without having done the strategy, she would have had to plan the entire book again. Instead, she was able to go back to the document and redesign the topic of the book, as per the new norms brought in by the COVID pandemic, without having to waste a lot of time on it. Because the strategy document was there, already developed, she could simply look at it and adjust it. Instead, she ended up with an Amazon #1 Bestseller.

A perfect example of the power of good strategy is that of Professor Christian Farioli. Typical of many thought leaders, he had amassed an incredible career in digital marketing spanning almost two decades. He had been an early adopter when it came to the marketing opportunities on the Internet, and the idea of writing a book had been percolating in his head for quite some time. He had just one problem: "I always have a lot of ideas, and once I start writing them down, out comes a massive, massive amount of content. It was a problem, because you don't want to read an encyclopaedia. You want to read a book," Christian said. "I needed the help of someone who has been doing this for a long time, so they could help me channel the ideas in one direction."

For Professor Christian, the key lay in good strategy. This focused him in on exactly who his readers were and the precise problem he could help them solve. He was then able to connect this with his Italian heritage and write "The Pizza Guide to Digital Marketing" which was detailed, actionable and engaging. It even made the Amazon top bestsellers in its topic area!

Like Hanane and Professor Christian, you too can make your entire writing process easier if you come up with the strategy for your book first and then proceed to the other necessary elements to writing. Some of those things might change. You may see some of them differently when you really get into the book. But in each case, you'll be well served by having done the strategy.

START WITH STRATEGY

Developing a laser-focused strategy happens by starting from as big a picture as possible and then zooming in to get as hyper-focused as possible.

Bird's eye view of developing a strategy

In order to get an understanding of what you want your book to be about, focus on the following questions and try to answer them as thoroughly as you can.

- What is your life purpose?
- What **message / impact / legacy** do you want to share with the world?

....

....

....

....

- What/Who is your current target market?
- What is your ideal book topic? (You want to be super-focused on what you are best at — your niche. Do not be afraid of losing some of the "wrong" clients while making this choice; stand out as an expert to the right

audience on the right topic and the "right" clients will find you. Or, as John D Rockefeller said, *"Don't be afraid to give up the good to go for the great."*)

CHOOSING YOUR BOOK TOPIC

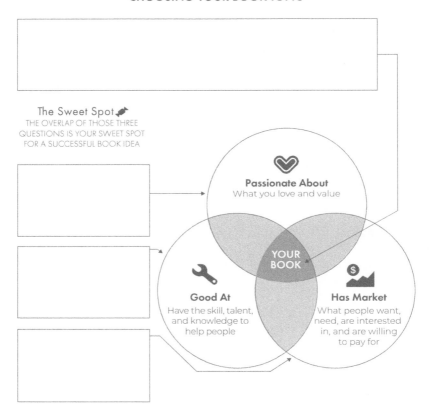

The Sweet Spot
THE OVERLAP OF THOSE THREE
QUESTIONS IS YOUR SWEET SPOT
FOR A SUCCESSFUL BOOK IDEA

Passionate About
What you love and value

YOUR BOOK

Good At
Have the skill, talent, and knowledge to help people

Has Market
What people want, need, are interested in, and are willing to pay for

- What is your primary goal in writing the book? *To become the leading authority on*

....

Now let's get crystal-clear on your ideal clients

What is better than having clients? Having clients you love!

With that in mind, answer the following question:

- Who *must* know about your book so that you get the results you want?

....

This question refers specifically to those clients who fulfil all three criteria mentioned (they WANT your services, they can INVEST, and you LOVE them). These clients will bring you ROI, either by way of publicity or by acquiring your services.

IDEAL CLIENT / AUDIENCE

Obviously, you want to serve as many people as possible. However, your resources will be limited, especially in the early stages. Focusing on those who serve you as much as you serve them will be crucial to your success.

Now, let's drill down deeper so we can identify your ideal client base.

- Demographics – Who are they/Where can we find them? (Below are some prompts. Not all of them may be applicable in your case; however, the more you know about your clients, the easier it will be to find them.)
  - Age
  - Gender
  - Family Status
  - Social Class
  - Cultural/Ethnic Distinctions
  - Income
  - Job/Career
  - Other....

- Psychographics – How do they think/What goes on inside their head?
  - Emotions
  - Values/Beliefs
  - Attitudes
  - Interests
  - Opinions
  - Group(s) they belong to

It's important to keep in mind that respecting people's culture and choices is key, yet from a marketing communications perspective it's important to tailor the messaging to fit the audience and you can only do that when you know exactly their demographics and psychographics.

Challenges and solutions

Now that you have a clear picture of your ideal client, let's think about the challenges they face and figure out how you can help. Keep your answers concise, ideally to no more than one sentence.

- What problem or aspiration do they have that you can help them with?

....

....

....

- How do you solve that problem or help them reach that aspiration?

....

....

....

- What is the real benefit of such an achievement?

....

....

- What is the biggest objection or doubt they may have?

....

....

....

....

- How do you overcome it?

....

....

....

....

- Why are you unique or better than your competition?

....

....

....

....

....

Develop your elevator pitch

It's now time to put it all together into a sharp and concise statement that commands attention and drives action, which is one of the most important aspects of your strategy. The elevator pitch is not only about your book; it's about what value you bring to the world at this stage. The elevator pitch will also be used as the basis for your book-cover content and book marketing materials. Use the structure below to focus your thoughts.

My book helps ....

.... (target audience)

Struggling with/aspiring to ....

.... (the problem or aspiration. Please note you only need one or the other)

Through ....

.... (how you solve the problem)

So they can ....

....(benefits they will get from reading the book)

Let's push things further and try to distil the elevator pitch into a one-line statement about what your book offers.

....

....

....

....

Typically, this could be a good basis for your book's subtitle.

All we are left with now is to come up with a great title for the book. This needs to be short, catchy and memorable. (At this stage, it's still a working title which you can change later once you get to the publishing stage.)

Working title for the book ....

....

....

Do not stress about your title and subtitle for now. You have plenty of time to figure them out (really, until the time you are ready to work on your book cover). I know from my experience working with authors that titles can change over the course of writing the book. Thus the *working* part of "working title": having even a working title means your mind has a goal to work towards.

Before we go further, I would like to give you an example of how strategy planning (especially defining the demographics and creating an elevator pitch for a very specific niche) helped our Author, Sarah Tabet, become an authority in her area. Sarah knew she wanted to write a book. She was a HR professional, but without good strategy she could easily get lost in a long list of other HR professionals who write books. So Sarah dug deep in the strategy session and really thought about the psychographics and demographics of who she wanted to reach, and the specific problem they needed help with. The result was her book, 'Inclusion Starts with U.' When other HR professionals were talking about inclusion as part of everything else in their portfolios, Sarah focused in on that and only that. Now, Sarah Tabet is recognised globally as a go-to thought leader on inclusion. She was even interviewed by global thought leader and bestselling author of *How Women Rise*, Sally Helgesen. Clarity in strategy, when met with clear and passionate content, meant Sarah was able to cut through the noise and reach global recognition in her niche.

Now that you know the ultimate purpose of your book and who it serves, it is time to decide what should go in the book.

Book outline

Let's zoom out and think of the book in totality and do a brain dump on all the topics you want to cover in the book (in no specific order). Picture your ideal client and imagine that you are giving a speech, presentation, or workshop to them. What topics would you want to share? What are the key points and major lessons you want to discuss/teach through the book?

If you've been working for a while and have taken your profession and career seriously — and why else would you be ready to write a book? — then you'll have lots of lessons to impart and plenty of points to make. The next step is to think about how you'll structure them. The best way is to organise your key points roughly into chapters:

- Use simple words to describe the chapter.
- You can combine several topics into one chapter.
- You can group several chapters into 2 or 3 sections if needed.
- The first chapter should ideally be your story (we use our proprietary Expert Positioning Story, which we will discuss in coming chapters).
- The second chapter will be a big-picture chapter, where you introduce new concepts or ideas you want to share with the world. If the concepts you are introducing are too big to fit in one chapter, you can split them as well. (The book you're reading is an example of that — the

second chapter introduced the "big why," while the third chapter focused on the "how".)

TOPICS TO BE COVERED IN THE BOOK

Picture your **ideal client/reader**, Just imagine that you are giving a speech, presentation, or workshop to them. if you are to teach them the most important things you learned,

What are the key points and major lessons you want to discuss / teach in the book?

ORGANISE THE KEY POINTS INTO CHAPTERS.

- ▸ Just use simple words to describe the chapter.
- ▸ You can combine several topics into one chapter.
- ▸ You can group several chapters into 2 to 3 sections if needed.

1. My story:
   Expert Positioning Story
	2. Big Picture Chapter
	   Mindset-Shift Chapter
		3.

4.	5.	6.
7.	8.	9.
10.	11.	12.

List the top 3-5 key messages you want to deliver in each chapter. Keep it short and to the point. For now, all you should write is the key message of the idea, not a full description.

Chapter	Top 3 - 5 key message / points
1. My story: Expert Positioning Story	
2. Big Picture Chapter Mindset-Shift Chapter	
3.	
4.	
5.	
6.	
7.	
8.	
9.	
10.	
11.	
12.	

IF YOU FAIL TO PLAN, YOU PLAN TO FAIL

Writing and publishing your book using this Guided Author System is so efficient that you can finish writing the content in about a month if you are focused. After that, publishing it takes an average of four months. All in all, your author journey could take from five to eight months, based on what I have seen from most authors. This is compared to using old-school ways of writing and publishing, which can take two to three years to see a book get from the author's brain to bookshelves.

Nonetheless, even the short process I am talking about can't happen without a proper project plan. The planning method I have come up with will allow you to manage your workload so you can hit your deadlines while still enjoying the process.

The planning process usually follows three steps:

1. Understanding what could delay your journey
2. Creating a project plan
3. Creating a celebration plan

Let's go through them one by one.

1. What Could Delay Your Journey?

My experience working with authors who are executives, leaders and entrepreneurs has shown me that the top three issues causing delays are:

You don't have time.

 You're confused about the process.

 You're not sure about your content.

These are all valid reasons, and they are all excuses.

 Don't have time? Everyone has the same 24-hour day. My team and I work with authors from all walks of life — parents, CXOs, professional experts and business owners. If they can do it, so can you.

It's about creating a project plan that works for you. Take into consideration all your other commitments and decide on a realistic pace that you can enjoy.

 Confused about the process? Keep it simple.
The Guided Author System is one of the most efficient author-creation systems. It takes all angles into consideration and is optimised to get the best output from the least input.

Furthermore, the content you create will be multi-use: content that serves you beyond the book for speeches, online courses, coaching manuals, blogs, etc.

If you follow the system step by step, you will get to your goal. If you try to reinvent the wheel, then you will only complicate your life.

 Not Sure About Your Content: All you need is 3000–3,500 words, or around 20 minutes of recording to come up with your basic content (it will take a total of 3-4 hours for the whole book, which is less than a half-day workshop).

Assuming you are an executive or leader with sufficient experience, coming up with relevant content using our system should be a walk in the park, even more so if you take part in our Guided Author program. You will work with a coach who will guide you, one on one, throughout the whole process.

Do not overcomplicate; trust yourself and keep it simple.

2. Prepare a Project Plan

Having a clear project plan for the whole journey will give you clarity on the commitments you need to make so you can manage your time wisely and, most importantly, enjoy the journey.

On the following page is my suggested format for planning.

Step	Estimated time requirements	Deadline

Creating Chapter Blueprints	Two-step approach:
	• Blueprinting session (up to 60 minutes per chapter)
	• Review & finalise (around 60 minutes per blueprint)
	  • *Total of 7-12 chapters depending on your chapter list*
	  • *Your first few blueprints will take around 90 minutes each*
	  • *Once you pass the third chapter, you should be able to work on two chapter blueprints per session*
	  • *Provision for any extra research time you might require*	

Full Blueprints Review	2-3 hours to conduct a full review and adjust all your blueprints	
Recording (or Writing)	**Recording:** 20 minutes of actual recording per chapter (total 7-12 recording sessions depending on your chapter list) **Writing:** If you are writing at an average writing pace, it will take you around 20 hours of actual writing	
Transcription (if recorded)	1 week on average, depending on which service you are using	
Review manuscript	If recorded: 8-12 hours total (within 1 week) If written: 4-6 hours to do a full readthrough (within 1 week)	

This would be the stage where your manuscript is ready. Then you need to chalk out the deadlines for the cover, bells and whistles (those other items apart from the content that complete your book), as well as the publishing.

Step	Deadline
Writing your book cover content	
Beefing up your manuscript (bells and whistles): • Dedications • Acknowledgments • Introduction • Conclusion • Author bio • Services and CTAs (Call to Action) • Testimonials* * testimonials do take time, so it's ok to complete them during the publishing stage	
Publishing stage	Average timeline is 4 months

This is when your book is published. ITS TIME TO CELEBRATE

Before we talk about the celebration plan, though, here are a few more tips to help you get organised:

- Put the sessions and deadlines you have planned in your calendar. This will allow you to book time to finish them, otherwise life will take over and you will miss your deadlines.
- Create a folder on your computer and call it "my book" so you can find all relevant files when you need them.
- Create a bookmark tag on your browser so you can save any relevant content that might be useful in creating your content.

3. Celebration Plan

This is the celebration you're going to have when you officially publish your book. You are going to go out there and have fun in whichever way you enjoy most, because you have earned it.

Use the celebration template on the next page: set the target completion date; even better, fill in the exact time, too. Then start thinking about where you want to celebrate your book. Just close your eyes for a moment and take a deep breath. Where are you when you're celebrating? It could be at home, it could be with friends, it could be in a restaurant, it could be in a club. No matter where you want it to be, write it down.

Then think of who you are with. Write down all the minor details that come to your mind. What are you actually doing?

Close your eyes. What do you see? "Oh, I'm dancing!" Well then, write "Dancing."

What do you see when you're there? Look around you in your head. You may think, "Oh my God, my whole family is here. I see my family celebrating with me. I hear sounds of spoons and forks and people eating. I smell... *mmm*... hot cooked food, and I taste... *mmm*... my favourite dish. And I feel proud and excited that I am celebrating my passion!" Write it down, making it as deeply detailed as you can. Conjure up the specifics.

Then write any other descriptions that come to you. Your celebration plan should be vivid in your mind.

Use the celebration template on the next page to make your celebration vivid. Then do what it takes to make it real. To help you visualise this, I have also created a Passion Journey Meditation that you can download at https://passionpreneurpublishing.com/free-book-resources

At .... : .... am/pm on .... /. .... /20 .... I'm celebrating holding my book in my hands

I'm at ....

With ....

Doing ....

I see ....

I hear ....

I smell ....

I taste ....

I feel ....

Working on the strategy and planning for your book is just the first step on the journey to becoming an author, but not doing it carefully and thoughtfully can have a great impact on your book and your experience creating it. Do as much blueprinting as you can, and make sure that you keep referring back to these documents as you advance through the journey.

ARE YOU INTERESTED OR ARE YOU COMMITTED?

As I said earlier, "interested" is a good way to describe you when you go to the movies. Unfortunately, having a short attention span is one of the downsides of the new social media world. Flipping, swiping and double-tapping can be the limits of some people's commitments. You need to be more than interested in your book journey. You need to be truly committed to it.

If you recall, in the previous chapter we talked about the three qualities of a successful leader: courage, humility and discipline. I find that discipline tends to be the hardest for most people.

You now have a clear strategy. You know your niche market. You have a sharp book elevator pitch and you have a solid project plan. All that is left is execution. Just follow the system step by step: like so many of our successful authors, you will get to your celebration date.

One of the great examples I like to give here was one of our very first authors, Mona Al Hebsi. I will never forget the look in her eyes the day I met her at our sales seminar; it was almost as if she could see herself as an international author. "Will you help me write and publish my book," she asked, "and how long will it take?" The next thing she did was pull out her credit card! She was committed!

Her level of commitment meant she had the courage to share her vulnerabilities and concerns, the humility to ask for the help she needed, and most importantly the discipline to stick with the process and timelines. The result? She was published in less than six months from the day we met her at the seminar.

The next step is creating your book blueprints, which is the topic of our next chapter.

 **Well done!**
Time to reward yourself.

CHAPTER

5

BLUEPRINTING

The Best Way to Outline a Book

BLUEPRINTING

The Best Way to Outline a Book

"STRUCTURE IS MORE IMPORTANT THAN CONTENT IN THE TRANSMISSION OF INFORMATION."

— ABBIE HOFFMAN

ORGANISED KNOWLEDGE IS POWER

Let me return to an idea I used earlier: Imagine building a high-rise without having proper architectural drawings and engineering plans. Would you want to live in such an unplanned tower?

Blueprints are just as important to the structure of a book as they are to a building. They're the skeleton that will carry the rest of the body. Without the blueprints, your thoughts will remain scattered; that will bring more confusion than clarity to the content-creation stage and make the outcome less satisfactory. Blueprinting is an important step to follow, whether you prefer to type or record your content.

In this chapter, you will learn about the main kinds of blue-prints, which type of content each of them works best for, and how to utilise them to organise your thoughts.

WHAT ARE BLUEPRINTS AND HOW DO I USE THEM?

Outlining a book has been a standard part of successful book writing projects for a long time. This old-school method is very good for professional writers who have the book's structure clearly in mind. But for those who are subject-matter experts but not writers, people like you and me, outlining can be tedious and time-consuming.

For today's author, who knows their content and would like a modern-day solution that works hand in hand with technology, we have developed a blueprinting system to organise your thoughts and create a solid backbone for your book.

Blueprints are documents through which you introduce a bird's-eye view of what you are going to talk about in each chapter and develop a flow from one chapter to the next. This is a much more practical process when you are at the content creation stage, because you can simply move things around from one chapter blueprint to the next until you feel the storyline is flowing smoothly. And, it means you have a more impactful book when it gets to the reader.

One of the authors I've worked with, Dr Kasem Akhras, serves as a great example of how blueprints helped him finish a book in just about a month. When he approached me, he had his material ready in the form of PowerPoint presentations. He had an idea and a vision for his book — how the chapters would flow, and how the information would be presented. The blueprints we developed together helped him structure his chapters and gave a better flow to the whole book. He filled in his blueprints using his prepared material, which gave him a clearer picture of what content was important and what was not.

The other beauty of Dr Kasem's blueprints, and in fact any of the blueprints created by our authors and coaches, is that it shows you where all your content needs to be. You then know which stories have been used, which statistics and graphs you need, and you can pace the whole book in a way that isn't rushed and overloaded in sections while being light on and dragged out in others. You are able to prioritise and map it all out in a way that makes sense. This is what Dr Kasem did.

In other words, if you think about the strategy work for your book as a view from 30,000 feet, the blueprints offer a 15,000-ft. view: closer to the final product, yet still high enough to allow you to pivot and adjust until you are happy with the big picture.

On average, you should not spend more than an hour per chapter outline. All you need to do is set out the content in bullet points. Even if you are going to type instead of recording, we strongly recommend that you write the key bullet points first and then populate the content in the following stage. Otherwise, you could run the risk of drowning in your own content.

From my extensive research, I have discovered that the majority of transformational book content fits into 3 main sections. Each requires a blueprint, totalling 3 types of blueprints:

A. Expert-Positioning Story: This is where you tell your story in a way that positions you as an expert in the eyes of your target audience. (This would be similar to the first chapter of this book, where I shared my story as an author and publisher.)

B. Mindset-Shift Chapters: These are simply "The Big Picture" chapters where you introduce new concepts to generate Aha! moments. These would be similar to the previous few chapters in this book (as well as this one) where I introduced you to methodologies you might not have come across before. Typically, you will have one Mindset-Shift Chapter, but there could be more, given back-to-back (as in Chapters 2, 3, 4 and 5 in this book); or you might even have a chapter that comes between those with new concepts in the middle of the book. This really depends on the overall structure of your book, which we tackled in the strategy section.

C. Teaching Chapters: This is the optimal format for the rest of the content in your book, where you teach the lessons, roadmaps or guiding points you want to share in a simple, structured manner.

There are two ways to start forming your blueprints: either start with your Expert Positioning Story and build up from there; or work on your Mindset-Shift Chapter, build your Teaching Chapters, and then narrate your Expert Positioning Story. Personally, I prefer to start from the story (if you are clear on what personal story you want to tell) as this acts as a guideline for the rest of the book. However, we have worked with authors who know precisely what new concept they want to introduce, so they start with a Mindset-Shift Chapter, map out the lessons and then go back and figure out which angle in their personal history is most relevant.

We are going to dive deeper and explain each of them on the coming pages.

A. Expert Positioning Story (EPS):

One of the cornerstones to spreading your message and building your personal brand is your own story. A well-told story is one of the most powerful tools to connect with your audience — if you get it right.

But the question is: how do you tell your story in a way that positions you as an expert? This is where the Expert Positioning Story framework comes into play.

The EPS will show the audience that you are NOT just another "theory" person — that you know your stuff and you can save them time, energy and money getting the results they want to get. It establishes you as a role model, someone who is an expert on the subject, with real-world experience, someone who has walked the talk and can guide others on the same path.

So, how did the EPS come about?

The EPS isn't something that was developed overnight. It was designed from:

- Meticulous research in PR and Communications
- Analysing the world's top speakers and authors
- Studying the Dramatic Arc used in storytelling, best-selling movies and plays

- Studying the most successful platform-selling professionals
- My own experiences as a global speaker

Where can I use this EPS framework?

The best part of the EPS framework is that it can be used as more than just a first chapter. By developing it for your book, you are creating a core element for everything else you choose to do as a thought leader: inspirational talks and speeches, online webinars, blogs, courses, social media marketing (SMM), platform selling, as well as your LinkedIn and author bios.

TELL YOUR STORY IN A WAY THAT POSITIONS YOU AS AN EXPERT... EXPERT POSITIONING STORY

Show the audience you are NOT just another "theory" person, you know your stuff and you can save them time, energy and money in getting them to the results they want to get to

Let me walk you through the structure and logic of EPS.

SECTION	WHY
Title / Subtitle / Chapter inspiration:	So they are intrigued & engaged with what the chapter is about
Start by sharing your **struggle**	Show reader you have been through what they are going through and you understand their pain (me too!). You are NOT just another "theory" person, you have walked the talk
Share **attempts** of trying to find a solution	
Share your realisations & **AHA! Moments**	Create drama, emotional moments
Share **results** you got for **yourself**	Create anticipation so the reader thinks in their head "I want that too!"
Why we should care about you (your purpose)	So people connect with your true passion, purpose & cause
Why we should **consider you the expert** (sources of knowledge)	So people know that you can teach (being able to teach is totally different from doing it for yourself, it requires an advanced level of knowledge)
Share **stories of success for your clients** and customers	Social proof that you can deliver what you are promising
The very specific problem you solve (**book elevator pitch**)	Simplify what you offer and get them excited to continue reading
Bridge: How this links to the topic of the coming chapter	Segue for a smooth transition to next chapter

Since the EPS is usually something intensely personal, you might find the words flowing. So, it's okay to write this immediately, within the dedicated space, rather than doing a blueprint first and then content. Either way, please follow the below blueprint structure.

THE EXPERT POSITIONING STORY BLUEPRINT

Title: Must be attractive and short. If your life was a movie, what would it be called?

....

....

Subtitle: This should give a clear, short and simple explanation of what's in the chapter.

....

....

Chapter inspiration: An inspiring quote, a question to the reader, a shocking statement, or anything that grabs the attention of the reader (relevant to the chapter). Remember that blueprinting is outlining. You need only to put down dot points that you can expand on later.

....

....

....

Note: Inspiration can be added at the end of the writing journey

First, start by sharing your struggle. Keep your story within the general context of how you are trying to position yourself as an expert. Start by talking historically, from as long ago as is relevant. Share your realisations and Aha! moments. Think of your "light-bulb moment" – when it dawned on you why all the older, available solutions would not work or had failed to work for you. Be specific in your examples and don't shy away from emotion. This lets the reader connect with you and your journey.

Share your struggle: Share your frustrations, attempts at finding success, and the light-bulb moment when you realised why other approaches didn't work.

....

....

....

....

....

Next, you want to get the audience excited about the success you have achieved so they become interested and want to know more. Sharing your journey, your frustration and then your results is a powerful way to do this because it creates connection and engagement with your readers. They want to know you solved the problem they are facing.

Share your successes: What are the results you have achieved for yourself? How did you solve the problem your reader is facing?

....

....

....

....

Now, your reader needs to know why they should care about you. This is a good time to talk about your purpose and why they should consider you the expert. Describe your sources of knowledge to demonstrate why you know more than the average expert (this includes certifications, degrees, years of experience, achievements etc.).

Explain your credibility: What is your purpose and vision? What are your qualifications, or areas of expertise?

....

....

....

....

Next, share any relevant stories of success that you have been able to realise for your clients and customers. This is a powerful way to add credibility, as it shows your results can be replicated in the lives of other people.

Share your client and customer successes:

....

....

....

....

Before you end the expert positioning story chapter, talk about the very specific problem you solve in this book. This is basically a rephrasing of the book elevator pitch you developed in your strategy session.

Share a rephrased version of your elevator pitch:

....

....

....

....

Finally, end the chapter with a bridge that links it to the topic of the coming chapter. To make it easier, let me give you a few sentence starters that you can use as a segue:

- "This leads us to…"
- "All this means that…"
- "There is an obvious need for…"
- "The next thing we will cover…"
- "The next topic to discuss…"
- "The next step will be…"

Choose a segue starter and complete it:

....

....

....

....

Now you have blueprinted the expert positioning story! All you need to do is take the dot points you created over the last few pages and, when it comes to content creation time, use them as talking points when you create your recordings.

Make sure you reward yourself!

Now let's blueprint the mindset-shift chapter.

B. Mindset-Shift Chapter (The Big Picture Chapter)

This is a pivotal chapter in your book. It is where you educate your audience about a new way of thinking — your way.

When you get this chapter right, you will cause a mindset shift in your audience, which is crucial. It clears their minds of any old learning, so they are ready to receive your teaching.

With the help of this chapter, you massage their minds and give them a feeling that makes them want more. Think about it as a one-chapter summary of the whole book. If you can nail this chapter, blueprinting the rest of the book becomes much easier. In some cases, this blueprint can also be used for a couple of other chapters in the middle of the book, to deliver a new concept.

For example, let's say your methodology includes three cornerstones, with a couple of steps under each, but those concepts require further explanation before diving into the teaching. You can use this blueprint to explain each of those cornerstones.

The best example to give here is my own book *Live Passionately – The Blueprint to Design a Life Truly Worth Living.*

The blueprint I created had 3 key sections:

- Section A: The Foundation of Going on a Passion Journey: Chapters 2 and 3
- Section B: Core Passion Chapters: Chapters 4, 5, and 6
- Section C: Passion Continuity Chapters: Chapters 7 and 8

For each of these sections, I used the Mindset-Shift blueprint to introduce the new concept, but then used the Teaching Chapter blueprint (to be introduced next) to explain that concept.

Keep in mind that this is only to be used in rare cases and only for two to three chapters, aside from Chapter Two; otherwise, the book will be filled with too many high-level concepts without introducing actual, executable steps.

The Big Picture chapter, along with your EPS, can be used as a lead magnet to get your audience excited enough about you and your methodology to go and buy your book.

In the blueprinting stage, it is important to keep it brief. That is why we just use dot points to cover the ideas and concepts that need to be fleshed out later in the writing/recording stage. However, as every part of the Guided Author System builds on the stage before it, we give indications as to how many words or minutes of recording will make up that section. These are indicated by an asterisk (*).

THE BIG PICTURE CHAPTER (BLUEPRINT)

* Word Count indication: 3,000 – 3,500 words/around 20 minutes of recording covering the below.

Title: Attractive and short

....

....

Sub-title: Clear and simple; what they will get from the chapter (optional)

....

....

CHAPTER SETUP

Hook: Start with an inspiring quote, a question to the reader, a shocking statement, or anything that draws the attention of the reader (relevant to the chapter)

* 50-100 words/less than a minute of recording.

....

....

Summary: Give a short summary of the topic to be discussed/taught in 1-2 paragraphs. Use sentences like "By the end of this chapter you will be able to…" OR "In this chapter you will learn…" OR "This chapter will enable you to…"

* 100–200 words/up to 1.5 min

....

....

MINDSET-SHIFT (WHY/WHAT)

Expose some misconceptions or explain the problem with the current situation

* 200-300 words/1-2 minutes

....

....

Provide a new way of looking at things, a light-bulb moment, and your point of view (provide any new definitions you want to present)

* 200-350 words/1-2 minutes

....

....

Share any evidence that supports your argument (facts/stats/stories)

* 200-300 words/1-2 minutes

....

....

EXPLAIN THE BIG PICTURE (THE HOW)

Roadmap: Give 5-10 key steps/pillars of your system/model/way
(you can group them into 2 to 3 groups of sub-points or sections if
you wish). Each of those steps will be explained in the succeeding
chapters of the book.

*1,000-1,500 words/6-10 minutes

CONCLUDE

Give the chapter summary (key takeaways from the chapter) and bridge to the next chapter

* 100–200 words/1-2 min.

....

....

Please note that you can write the keywords in the blueprint if they help you recall and construct longer sentences while actually recording or writing the book.

C. Teaching Chapters

After sharing your EPS and Big Picture chapters, you are now ready to instruct your audience, in a simple manner, so they can get from A to B using this blueprint.

The great news is that the same blueprint will be used for the remainder of the book, aside from any new major concept that you might introduce (which will need a Big Picture blueprint).

So, just treat each chapter with a fresh pair of eyes, and break it down per the provided blueprint, repeat it a few more times and you are done with blueprinting your book!

TEACHING CHAPTER BLUEPRINT

* Word Count indication: 3,000-3,500 words/around 20 minutes of recording

Title: Attractive and short; use the step name or learning pillar name introduced in the previous chapter

....

....

Sub-title: Clear and simple; what they will get from the chapter (optional)

....

....

CHAPTER SETUP

Hook: Inspiring quote, a question to the reader, a shocking statement, or anything that draws the attention of the reader (relevant to the chapter)

* 50-100 words/less than a minute

....

....

Summary: Give a short summary of the topic to be discussed/ taught in 1-2 paragraphs. Use sentences like "By the end of this chapter you will be able to..." OR "In this chapter you will learn..." OR "This chapter will enable you to..." (NOTE: use simple language, with or without a short headline)

*100–200 words/up to 1.5 minutes

....

....

....

....

....

....

CHAPTER CONTENT

Start with why: Answer the WIIFM question: *"What's In It for Me?"* Why is the information in this chapter important to learn? You can do this in any of the three ways below:

- Ask a powerful question to encourage reflection; use terms like "think about…" or "do you remember…" or "have you ever…"
- Tell a personal story that makes the reader understand the importance of your message.
- State the evidence backing up your argument.

Explain and teach: Explain what they need to know and teach them how to do it. Give a maximum of 3-5 points/steps and elaborate on each.

*1,000-1,500 words/6.5 to 10 minutes

....

....

....

....

....

....

Add supporting material: You can add visuals (graphs/charts), give a step-by-step example, include forms (templates or tables), and suggest further resources: blog articles, or downloadables (this can link back to your business/offer/website).

....

....

....

....

....

Relevant stories: You can add any stories from your personal or professional experience to help the reader understand the content of the chapter.

....

....

....

Conditions of success: Before concluding the chapter, you need to explore the ramifications and answer any objections (what if...?). You can use sentences such as, "For this to work you have to..." or "If you do not do... " or "This ...will not work because..."

....

....

....

....

CHAPTER CONCLUSION

Summary: List the key takeaways from the chapter

....

....

CTA: Call to Action. What should the reader think about or do as a next step (to apply the learning)?

....

Bridge: Segue to the next chapter, using this kind of sentence:

- "This leads us to…"
- "All this means that…"
- "There is an obvious need for…"
- "The next thing we will cover…"
- "The next topic to discuss…"
- "The next step will be… "

....

Remember, the bridge to the next chapter is optional, so don't force yourself to write it if it doesn't work.

Now that you've blueprinted one teaching chapter, you may go ahead and use this same system to blueprint all the others. Remember, this is like a recipe. Follow it to the letter in the beginning, and then you will learn what the ingredients are, and you may mix them up in your own way. While the chapter setup and conclusion elements need to stay where they are, you may want to introduce stories or supporting materials in with your key points or mix it up a little. As long as you don't skip any of the ingredients, and you keep the logical flow of the chapter, your recipe will turn out great.

GOOD WRITING IS A PRODUCT OF GOOD THINKING

Good writing is a product of good thinking, which is what the blueprints help you do. Remember, good does not necessarily mean "more"; it means "better".

Of course, you might realise that you need to do some research around specific sub-topics you are covering; blueprinting is the stage to conduct such research. Just be careful not to overdo it.

On average, you should not spend more than an hour per chapter blueprint; all you need to do is put the content in bullet points. If you are going to be typing instead of recording your content, I would still recommend that you put down your key bullet points first and then populate the content in the following stage. Otherwise, you run the risk of drowning in your own content.

FULL BLUEPRINT REVIEW

Once you are done with your blueprints, you should do an end-to-end review, from the beginning of your EPS all the way to the last chapter. Usually, I suggest printing the blueprints and putting them all on a table so you can see how the storyline flows. Are there any duplications/unnecessary repetitions, where things are mentioned in two chapters without added value? Is there a need to shuffle things around between chapters, or even combine some messages in certain chapters?

The concept behind blueprinting is that it is easy to shuffle, tweak, or alter your plan in order to ensure it covers everything it needs to cover and is well-paced and structured. It is not mandatory to make notes for each point mentioned in the blueprints. Sometimes you can tweak the blueprint and reorganise the elements based on your book topic and the tone of your writing.

But let me tell you, blueprints are a gamechanger.

Ashutosh Sinha, a global leader in HR with decades of experience at an executive level including inside a big 4 company, found this to be true. He knew he wanted to write a book, but had no idea of how to bring all the knowledge he held into a book that was less than the size of an encyclopaedia! This is what he said about his journey with Passionpreneur. "I had a story in my head that I had to tell to the world. But that was the easy part, the hard part was getting it down on paper. The key challenge was: How do I put my thoughts together? Writing a blog is easier. Writing an article is not so easy but not so hard. But writing a book was my biggest challenge. How do I get going on that? But when I met Moustafa from Passionpreneur, I was impressed with the fact that book writing is a science. And as we got talking, I realised that actually it's not about writing a book, but about living your experience in a way that is very structured."

Blueprinting, for Ashutosh, brought simplicity and clarity by mapping out exactly what was needed at every step of the way. It was no longer a daunting task. It was very simple, structured and achievable. The truth is that many people dream of becoming authors. The vast majority of them don't ever achieve this because it seems too difficult, convoluted or intimidating. Blueprinting offers simplicity and takes writer's block out of the equation by virtue of good planning. This has been the overwhelming benefit I've witnessed in the journeys of so many of our authors.

IN SUMMARY

Using the blueprinting system will ensure your messages are sharp, concise and effective. The Expert Positioning Story will help establish you as an expert/authority in your field. Big Picture Chapters will help shift the mindset of the readers, and work as a summary of the entire book, while the standard Teaching Chapters will help the audience navigate through the lessons in a smooth manner.

This means you are now ready to put meat on the bones, which is what we will cover in the coming step: Content Creation.

For now, well done!
Time to reward yourself.

CHAPTER

6

CONTENT IS KING!

The Content Creation Journey

CHAPTER 6

CONTENT IS KING!

The Content Creation Journey

"CONTENT IS KING."

— BILL GATES

PUTTING MEAT ON THE BONES

At this point, you have a laser-sharp niche, a focused strategy, and well-designed blueprints. It's now time to put meat on the bones.

Although this stage is typically the hardest in a book creation journey, if you use the Guided Author System I've been walking you through in this book, the entire process will be much easier. This is because you have the right structure in place.

By the end of this chapter, you will learn how to create your content in the most efficient way possible: either recording, if you are a natural-born speaker, or typing, if you are blessed with writing skills. Either way, by the end of this stage you will have the first draft of your book done. Exciting, right?

CONTENT IS KING

We all agree that content is king, but it is hard to produce it using old-school methods if you aren't crystal-clear about what to write about and how — especially if you are a first-time author. Without this kind of clarity, it is even harder to create content that is relevant, concise and impactful, which is the Holy Grail of any thought leader.

That is why I have simplified this process by using the top-down approach we've been discussing, from strategy through blueprints. By the time you have to create content, everything fits in place. Your messages will be concise and impactful; they will take your audience on a mental journey to the places you want them to go.

When Saahil Mehta came to us, he was already an excellent speaker and coach. His specialty was "helping leaders gain diamond-level clarity through identifying what was holding them back so they could de-clutter their life and scale their summits of success faster." The concept was well-developed as he was already presenting and working with this material. The next step was simply to take it and shape it into book form.

This is what I'm talking about when I say "content is king". Saahil had keen insight that was structured, focused, and already solving a problem for people! He used our blueprinting and coaching system to create his book, *Break Free*, which began opening doors for him straight away. Becoming an author increased his reach exponentially. But good content was the cornerstone of it all.

It's time for you to decide which method to use to create your content. As you know, I always record my books. I like it because it makes you feel like you're talking about your content to someone. Remember, I started out as a public speaker; I'm at my best when I'm explaining things verbally. I simply need to picture an audience when I make my recordings. You may find it works better to picture yourself talking to a close friend or a colleague, or even one of the people who work for you. As I mentioned earlier, a great thing about recording is that it tends to result in an interactive tone for the book.

But the more traditional method, typing, works just as well when you have already gone through the strategy and blueprints.

Let's now dive deeper into each approach.

OPTION A: YOUR VOICE, YOUR WORDS

*"SPEECH HAS POWER. WORDS
DO NOT FADE. WHAT STARTS OUT
AS A SOUND, ENDS IN A DEED."*

— ABRAHAM JOSHUA HERSCHEL

Think about it: most of us learned to speak before we learned to write, so, it's no wonder we find speaking easier than writing. That's why we have developed our "Your voice, Your words" system, which is a unique way to capitalise on your speaking ability.

Simply put, instead of writing down the first draft, you record yourself speaking based on the blueprints you have developed so far. You get it transcribed and your first draft is ready.

All you need to do is record an average of 20 minutes per chapter or a total of 3-4 hours of recording, which will end up producing around 30,000–35,000 words (a 150-to-180-page book).

Another advantage to recording your manuscript is that books created with this methodology literally sound like you. I recall that when I sent my last book to my niece, she called me and said, "When I'm reading, it's like you are with me in the room, I can hear your voice in my head." This is why it's important you speak in your most natural style and tone.

This is harder to achieve when you type. Our natural thought processes were created to be spoken, and it takes mental processing to figure out which combination of keyboard buttons to press to reproduce what we are trying to say.

To give you a better undertanding, let me tell you about Genevieve Pantin's experience with content creation. Genevieve had always been a natural observer of people, and had channelled this gift into a career as a psychologist and anthropologist. A chance meeting with Deepak Chopra made her realise the next step was to take her gift for observing, coaching and inspiring women, and then give it away. Her book, *A Lioness Heart*, was beginning to develop in her head. When she came to Passionpreneur, we took her on a journey of turning her wisdom into blueprints. She then recorded each of her chapters based on these blueprints. Each chapter needed about 20-25 minutes of recording which was later transcribed and reviewed before moving on to the next stage of publishing.

Managing to set some time aside every week, she recorded all her chapters, and in just weeks, the first draft of her manuscript was ready to go through the editing process. More importantly, Genevieve was on the way to elevating her practice as an elite coach and entrepreneur, and through that reaching more women.

Not every thought leader will have the time to spend hours, weeks or even months writing. Genevieve certainly didn't. Utilising the recording methodology meant she could focus on what she is good at, being a subject matter expert. And her writing skills were no longer an obstruction to becoming an international author and boosting her authority and credibility in her field.

I do need to make an important note on editing: Even if you send the manuscript to a professional editor, this is not ghostwriting. Again, I do not recommend ghostwriting because your voice may be overshadowed by the tone of the ghostwriter. It's important that you instruct any editors (including friends or family to whom you show your manuscript looking for feedback) not to try to change your natural tone.

Your tone includes your mannerisms, your metaphors and your ways of viewing the world. These are part of the powerful perspective you bring to the topic you've chosen to write about. Editing is there to clean up and polish language, not to make it less YOU.

HOW TO GO THROUGH THE "YOUR VOICE, YOUR WORDS" PROCESS

 1. Prepare

 2. Plan

 3. Record

 4. Organise

 5. Transcribe

1. Prepare

a. Print all your chapter blueprints; having it on paper makes it easier to navigate, move around, and add notes.

b. Time investment:

    i. You will need an average of 20 minutes per chapter.

    ii. Typically, each minute of recording generates about 155 words, depending on how fast you speak (the average range is 145 to 165 words per minute).

    iii. This generates a chapter of about 3,000–3,500 words for every 20 min recording.

    iv. Keep in mind that it's okay if some chapters are longer than others.

    v. Based on 7-12 chapters, the book will require an average of 2-4 hours hours of recording time.

    vi. This will easily produce a book with a word count of around 30,000 to 40,000 words, totaling 150–200 pages.

 2. Plan

a. Schedule the recording session times on your calendar to avoid missing deadlines.

b. Plan extra time for the first couple of sessions. They might take longer as you get used to the recording activity but should become easier as you progress.

c. Tools: you can use a computer, mobile phone or professional recorder. Below are some things to take into consideration:

i. Mobile phone:
- Most phones have recording apps. On the iPhone, it's called "Voice Memos" and on Android "Easy Voice Recorder" (you can download the Easy Voice Recorder from your Android's Google Play Store).
- Ideally, use a headset (it frees your hands, leaving you able to make additional notes on your blueprint, and produces a clearer sound recording).

ii. Computer
- Turn off all notifications or apps that make sounds or distract you; this includes emails, calendar, web browser, to-do reminders, etc.
- Software: On a Mac, you can use QuickTime player/file/new audio recording, or on Windows, you can use "Sound Recorder".

3. Record

a. Have your tools ready (chapter blueprints, recording tool and headset). Also make sure to have some water next to you, in case your throat feels dry.
b. Make sure you put your phone in "flight mode" when you are recording so you do not get calls or notifications.
c. Find a quiet space and make it clear to people around you that you do not want to be interrupted; avoid distractions (this is important for your flow).
d. Choose the tone you want to speak with:

  i. Conversational, as though conversing with a friend.

  ii. More formal, as though helping a stranger heal the same pain you had.

 e. Grab your chapter blueprint and start speaking, starting with the chapter title:

  i. Think about who the ideal audience is for this book and pretend that you are talking to them. Go back to the ideal audience / niche you worked on during the book strategy session. If you can picture a real person you know who fits the mould, that will make it even easier.

  ii. Follow the blueprint structure *(say the chapter number and name so when you get the manuscript, you know which document belongs to which chapter).*

  iii. If you have any charts, graphs or images to be inserted in the chapter, then mention them when their place comes in the script. For example, as you are recording the chapter, say, "Insert chart 3 here".

  iv. Speak naturally and normally, and make sure your voice is clear. Use your own words; you do not have to follow the blueprint word for word.

  v. Do not worry if the words do not come out right every time; you can make changes when you get the transcripts.

 f. Always remember to breathe. It will keep you relaxed and clear your thoughts.

4. Organise

a. Save each recording with the number and name of the chapter.

b. Put all the files in one folder (name it per the book title or working title).

5. Transcribe

a. If you are using our services, simply zip the file, send it to your account manager and they will do the rest. We guarantee 99% accuracy in transcripts.

b. If you are doing it yourself, you have a few options:

   i. Use freelancers online on sites like Fiverr.com or more high-end transcription services. The more professional the service, the more expensive it is and the better quality of transcription you get.

   ii. Use transcription software (typically the accuracy rate is around 80%, which means you have to do more work cleaning it up).

OPTION B: TYPING

*"ALL I NEED IS A SHEET OF PAPER AND
SOMETHING TO WRITE WITH, AND THEN
I CAN TURN THE WORLD UPSIDE DOWN."*

— FRIEDRICH NIETZSCHE

Some people are blessed with writing skills; they enjoy writing or feel comfortable with typing. If this is you, then it might be easier for you to type your manuscript than record the content. Additionally, sometimes the type of content you are trying to produce might be too technical to record. It might be easier for you to type so you can see it as you are progressing.

The most important thing is to make sure you follow the blueprints, as this will help keep your thoughts organised and the content well-structured.

Typing typically takes longer than recording (though it takes less time to clean up). To help you estimate your writing workload, anticipate up to 20 hours of actual content creation. Keep in mind this depends on many variables, such as your typing speed, the duration of your typing sessions, and whether you write the chapters in one session or need to redraft.

REVIEW AND CLEAN UP

*"THE FIRST DRAFT REVEALS THE ART;
REVISION REVEALS THE ARTIST."*

— MICHAEL LEE

The most important thing to consider when choosing between recording or typing is what comes more naturally and is more comfortable. If you are unsure what method to go with, do a small sample of each to see what works better. Either way, you will need to review and clean up the file before the manuscript goes on to the publishing stage.

During the review and cleanup stage it is normal to correct, add, remove or adjust the content. Take your time; it's a major milestone to have your manuscript ready to go to publishing, so do not rush it.

EXPANDING YOUR CONTENT AND NETWORK!

Two minds are better than one. If you have access to other experts and thought leaders, then you surely want to capitalise on that to make your book even better.

When you work with a professional publisher with author networks, you have the advantage of connecting with fellow authors and collaborating with them on the content of your book, if it is relevant. This can occur in the form of quotes, insights, or interviews.

When I formed Passionpreneur Publishing, I made sure all the authors who worked with me had access to each other as well. A great example to use here is Abdalla Nasr who cross-interviewed me, our bestselling author Pegah Gol and several other authors for his book *The Corporate – The Art of Thriving in a Competitive Talent Market.* The result was a book that brought a lot of professional points of view, got support from the authors interviewed and hit an Amazon #1 bestseller on the week of its launch.

Now, if you are following along with this process as I explain it to you, then you are done with all the heavy lifting. You deserve a big 'Well done!' You have reached a major milestone, completing the first draft of your book.

So go on and celebrate, and when you are ready, move to the next chapter, where we will explain how you can move up to the next level in your journey as a published author.

Well done!
Time to reward yourself.

7

BELLS AND WHISTLES

We All Like a Little Extra

CHAPTER 7

BELLS AND WHISTLES

We All Like a Little Extra

IS YOUR CAR THE BASIC MODEL OR DELUXE?

What's the difference between a basic car and a deluxe model? The basic car won't change the duration of the trip, but the deluxe model will surely make the journey smoother and more impressive – both during the drive and when you show up at your destination. Remember, your book needs more than just the learning content you've worked so hard so far to provide. Think of this as the icing on the cake.

I like to call these features the 'Bells and Whistles' as they are all the extras that help gain more attention, increase credibility and drive your Call to Action (CTA), so you get the maximum Return On Investment (ROI) for your book.

Before I delve deeper into what the bells and whistles are and how to go about creating them, I want to talk about how Dr. Omar Fisher's bells and whistles added additional zest to the book he was writing. His book, *Conscious Wealth*, was already highly practical as he had designed it to be an actionable playbook for transforming your relationship with money. But adding bells and whistles meant it became a gateway to higher engagement as well.

The introduction and conclusion were crafted to help Dr. Omar's readers understand why and how they should read his book and what to do after they finished it. They were shown how to access his website to get access to more events, webinars or even coaching. The author bio, testimonials and call to action pages helped build his credibility and let the readers know about his services. The book was good on its own, but as Omar added in these sections, it gave context, anticipation and added excitement to his message.

One of the most powerful sections when it comes to bells and whistles is the testimonial section. Here, readers begin to see how other people benefit from the author's work. It creates something marketers call "social proof." It's that feeling of "Oh, if other people trust this person, I can, too." One of our authors, Dr. Sweta Adatia, used this strategy expertly with her book, *Future Ready Now,* which harnessed cutting-edge neuroscience and applied it to career planning for families and education providers. The testimonials, and the extras Dr. Sweta added in, created the social proof beautifully with big names offering their support. The result was a book that made you anticipate good results if you picked it up and used it.

It's been said many a time by authors in the Passionpreneur tribe that 'your book is your business card.' An essential part of this lies in the bells and whistles section. The extras you offer can drive people to your website or to engage with your other services. Do you have coaching options, online courses or speaking offerings? What else do you offer for your readers and how can they access you? This is a powerful generator for extra ROI as you use your book to open doors of opportunity. I used this strategy with my own book, *Live Passionately*. In the bells and whistles section, I offered people access to a free passion meditation they could access on my website, along with other tools and infographics that would help them lead a passionate life. Not only does it increase engagement and ROI, but it creates trust as the reader gets more from you than just the book they purchased.

It's not just Dr. Sweta, Dr. Omar or even me; many authors who've worked with me have managed to get an ROI on their books in this way. Remember, the bells and whistles supercharge your book and contribute to getting more clients, building credibility and becoming an authority in your field.

SO, WHAT ARE THE BELLS AND WHISTLES?

Here are the most important things you need to add to your manuscript:

 1. Testimonials

 2. Dedication

 3. Acknowledgements

 4. Book Introduction

 5. Conclusion

 6. Author Bio

 7. Your Offer

Let's go through them one by one:

1. Testimonials

No one likes to blow their own trumpet, and it doesn't have the same credibility as praise from a third person. The impact of you saying "I'm the greatest" is worlds apart from *someone else* saying that about you.

Testimonials consist of quotes that say something positive about you or your book. They can come from any of the following sources:

- Quotes from credible, high-status people (this requires that you have a strong relationship with these people so you can ask for testimonials)
- Press mentions
- Reader and customer feedback
- Fellow authors/coaches/speakers

Before you go out to get some testimonials, let me give you a few insider tips.

- **Get testimonials about you rather than about the book:** These are much easier to get — as opposed to asking someone to read your whole book so they can say something about it. (The likelihood is that if they do not know you well enough to give a testimonial about *you*, then they will not give one about your book anyway.) Testimonials about you can be used on your website, social media and even as blurbs on future books.

- **Reach out to fellow authors:** Capitalise on the community. An author is a credible figure who will make for a credible testimonial. This also opens up room for collaboration between you and them.

How many testimonials should I get and where do I place them?

It's great to have as many testimonials as you can get. You can have a few pages at the beginning of the book full of testimonials. You can also get 1-2 quality testimonials from credible figures or fellow authors — those are the only ones worth putting on the back cover (your cover is premium property so every word must be worth its space).

Keep in mind that testimonials might take time to arrange. I suggest you initiate this activity first, before you get on with the rest of the bells and whistles. Ideally, you want to submit all the testimonials that will go inside the book along with your manuscript for editing. You can give yourself a bit longer for the one or two testimonials that will go on the back cover if you are waiting for someone very high-profile. In that case, make it clear to your publishers so they can allocate space for it while doing the cover design.

2. Dedication

The dedication usually goes on the dedication page, which is at the very front of the book, after the title page.

A book dedication, as the name suggests, is your way to honour someone. This could include your parents, siblings, life partner, children, someone to whom you really owe a lot to, or even the readers or the community at large.

Take time to choose who you are dedicating your book to and then write a few words from the heart. Keep it short and sweet.

3. Acknowledgements

This section is where you recognise and thank everyone who helped you with your book. It's a way to display your appreciation for them in a public and permanent form. This can include all of those who helped you on the journey of making the book happen — your friends, extended family members, coaches and mentors, business associates, publishing team members involved in the book process, etc.

The acknowledgements section will also create stronger relationships with the people who helped you in this journey; when people feel their support is appreciated in such a public manner, they will support you even further.

For this one, there is no specific template. It's as simple as, "I would like to acknowledge person ABC for their support in XYZ." Just take a few moments to reflect on your journey, think of everyone who helped you make it happen, and list their names and what they helped you with.

4. Book Introduction

Writing your introduction is going to be a useful exercise to help you distil your ideas and encapsulate the message of your work in a few short paragraphs.

The second goal of your introduction is to intrigue the readers enough to buy your book. These two purposes, distilling your ideas and intriguing your readers, will serve as the basis for your back-cover content — where you'll need your most compact and powerful message.

The introduction can range from 450 to about 1,000 words. You can use the below blueprint to help you write your intro.

BOOK INTRO BLUEPRINT

An inspiring quote, a question to the reader, a shocking statement, or anything that draws their attention (relevant to the intro's contents)

....

....

Acknowledge the reader

....

....

Start with why they should read the book, and why it is important

....

....

What is the most interesting story or claim in the book?

....

....

What is the story people always ask you about?

....

....

What sentence or fact makes people sit up and take notice?

....

....

What is the intended audience going to care about the most or be most interested in or shocked by?

....

....

Summarise the current pain point (Ask a question)

....

....

Outcome/solution: Guide them to imagine/visualise an inspiring outcome this book can bring to their life

....

....

....

Learning: Tell them the top 3-5 learnings this book offers

....

....

....

Credentials: Talk about your background/credentials

....

....

....

Purpose: Talk about what purpose you want to serve with this book (no one cares about you, really. What they care about is What's In It For Me)

....

....

....

What it's not: What the book is, and what it is not

....

....

....

Bridge to the first chapter, the Expert Positioning Story: a simple transition to get the reader curious to read your personal story.

....

....

....

5. Conclusion and Call to Action

The conclusion should clearly summarise the book. Address any lingering issues and close any open loops, but make sure you don't introduce any new concepts or give out any new information here.

You can point the readers to additional resources you have that could help them. You should also include a call to action of some sort. In essence, tell the reader what to do after closing the book.

Do NOT:
- Do not introduce any new content. This should only be a summarisation of what is in the book and a call to action.

You can use the blueprint on the next page to help you write the conclusion.

BOOK CONCLUSION BLUEPRINT

Summarise the top 3-5 takeaways from the book

....

....

Restate the book's mission

....

....

Tell them you want to hear from them if they have any questions or require further assistance (refer to your contacts in "about the author")

....

....

CTA: What should the reader do when they finish the book? When they read the last word and put the book down, what is the first thing you want your reader to do? The underlying message is straightforward and empowering: now that you have all the tools, go out there and use them.

....

....

6. Author Bio

Remember, your book is your business card. So, it is very important to share your bio in the book. For a good Author Bio, you can make use of the guidelines below:

- Demonstrate your authority and credentials on your book subject (but don't overstate them).
- Include achievements that build credibility or are interesting to the reader (without going overboard).
- Mention any other books you have written, or training programs, online courses and workshops you have conducted.
- Drop some relevant names if they are appropriate (without being a show-off).
- Share something personal about you (hobbies).
- Add your contact details (website/email/social media handles).

 ## 7. Your Offer

All our Passionpreneur authors love to share, teach and support their audience. So, sometimes we find ourselves having more to offer than can fit in a book... sounds familiar?

That is a great challenge to have, which brings us two opportunities:

- If your material is more like worksheets, guides, checklists, etc., then create a downloadable pack to use on your website as another lead magnet or as supporting material for your workshops and coaching.
- If your extra material is a lot more than just that, great, you have another book in you. Keep those notes handy so you can use them when you start writing your next book. I hope you didn't think your first book would be your last! If anything, it's the beginning of your journey towards becoming a Global Thought Leader. Authors like Dr Marshall Goldsmith and Brian Tracy have published in excess of 30 books each.

You can start working on the bells and whistles as soon as you are done with your content creation. Ideally, these sections should be in the manuscript when it goes for editing.

While your content is the soul of your book, the bells and whistles make it more interesting and give it a complete, embellished finish. So, make sure you set enough time aside to work on the bells and whistles once you are done with the main chapters of your manuscript.

You have now finished producing the content of your book. The heavy lifting is done. The weight is off your shoulders, and now it's the responsibility of the publisher to turn your manuscript into an internationally published book, which is what we will discuss in the coming chapters.

**Well done!
Time to reward yourself.**

CHAPTER

8

TURN YOUR MANUSCRIPT INTO A BOOK

Let's Talk Publishing

TURN YOUR MANUSCRIPT INTO A BOOK

Let's Talk Publishing

"TRUTH, LIKE GOLD, IS TO BE OBTAINED NOT BY ITS GROWTH, BUT BY WASHING AWAY FROM IT ALL THAT IS NOT GOLD."

— LEO TOLSTOY

THE SECOND STAGE OF YOUR BOOK JOURNEY

You are finally done with the heavy lifting. What an achievement! From here on, your role switches to mostly reviewing and approving. The publishing stage is where you take your manuscript and turn it into an actual book.

In this chapter, I am going to introduce the different publishing options available in the market and explain which among them is more suitable to which target audiences. I am going to show you the key stages in the publishing process and how to plan a successful publishing journey, from editing all the way to global distribution.

WHAT ARE MY PUBLISHING OPTIONS?

Let's zoom out for a bit to understand your publishing options.

Traditional publishing, as the name implies, is the way all publishing used to work. Then disruptive innovation in technology enabled **self-publishing**, which is great for DIY lovers but does not solve the problem of certain niches like busy leaders, which then brought to life Indie and executive publishers like Passionpreneur Publishing.

Lets elaborate on each of them one by one.

Traditional Publishing

Traditional publishers depend on a high-volume model, both in choosing authors and in selling. Typically a traditional publisher will spend a lot of time looking for sellable content. Once it is accepted, the publisher takes over your manuscript, turns it into a book and puts it on the shelves. This process also takes many, many months, as there is often a long line of titles in the pipeline. It all happens with zero financial investment from the author.

On the plus side, traditional publishing offers the following:

- You do not have to invest money to publish your book
- A little money up-front. (Only in the case of you being an established celebrity in your field)
- Some prestige, depending on the publisher you sign up with
- Offers bookstore distribution support (which is the main value of traditional publishers)

It works best for:

- Established celebrities with a big following
- Full-time writers who write for a living
- Fiction (novels)

Like everything, traditional publishing has its flip side too. So, what are the trade-offs?

- Pitching your idea: There is a lot of work involved to reach out to publishers, like preparing book proposals, a pitch document that presents why your book (idea) is salable and marketable in today's market. Your work is not done once you are finished writing. The publisher outreach by itself becomes another project.
- Need for a third party: You will usually need a literary agent, who also takes a cut, to do the publisher outreach for you.

- Waiting time: It takes around 3-6 months to hear back from a good traditional publisher, and unless the publishers thinks your book is going to be in demand and has immediate potential for sales, the answer is often a polite no.
- Lots of leg work: You will need to reach out to a lot of publishers, that's why you hear stories about authors reaching out to tens of publishers before getting a yes.
- Loss of control: Even if you get a yes, you will most likely lose control of your book. Traditional publishers basically tell you what and what not to write; they even decide what goes on the cover. It's only fair, since they are taking the financial risk on it, but it's not so good if you want control over the destiny of your book. Simply put, the publisher's focus is to make their money back, even if at times that means going against your wishes.
- Time to market: Traditional publishers take a long time to publish. It takes 9-18 months before your book hits the shelves.
- Low ROI: Most of the time it is not financially rewarding (especially for non-fiction books); statistically, 75% of books do not even cover their break-even costs; either way, you only get a fraction of the money, only 3-5% of your book's sale price. So, you do the math and figure it out.

With so much time wasted and the high probability of low revenue, we can confidently say that the old model is broken (at least for leaders, entrepreneurs and executives who value their time and freedom in making their own decisions).

Self-Publishing

In the same way tech disruption created Uber in the taxi industry, tech disruption created the ability to self-publish. This DIY style has surely shifted the power of publishing to the author's hands. You own 100% of your copyright, decision-making... and headache!

Who is it for?

- Those who enjoy the artistic process of publishing and working on a lot of minor details of the book journey
- Those who need to save money at the expense of time (typically if you are still at the beginning of your career, so your time has very low value compared to your income)

On the downside:

- You will waste a lot of time in trial and error to clearly scope each step of the publishing journey and then find and recruit the right team members. Often you will find that they only do part of the job and leave you hanging halfway through till you find the next person to fill in the blank
- When you eventually make it to the end, your book will have no credible publisher's name associated with it
- You may struggle to compete with other self-published authors out there, as there is a sea of content all with varying quality, visual appeal and credibility attached to it

Independent Publishing

This is known as "Indie" publishing, and it is where our Passionpreneur Publishing fits in.

First and foremost, most indie publishers are "niche", which means they focus on authors who have a specific area of expertise or follow a particular genre. A lot of them have unique revenue models; some work purely on fixed fees, and others have a mix of fixed fees plus royalties.

The other advantage of indie publishers is that, due to their size, it is very likely you'll end up dealing with the owners or most senior leadership, which doesn't happen often when you are dealing with major-league publishers. This is useful if you want an ongoing relationship with your publisher or want some special handling of your project.

Who is it for?

- You have a specific niche and prefer to deal with teams familiar with your book genre
- You want 100% control over your book
- You prefer a personalised relationship with your publisher

On the downside:

- You are going to have to invest in your own book, which should not be an issue if you are a successful leader, but is a problem for those early in their career journey

- Credible indie publishers are hard to find, and even if you find them their niche might not be a good fit for you
- Because these are fairly non-standard publishers, their deals are also not standard, so make sure you are clear on what you are getting for your money
- Be aware that some organisations that appear as Indie publishers are colloquially called "vanity publishers" in the industry. They are forever upselling you to the next thing that they claim will make your book a hit. But you will be out of pocket with unforeseen expenses, and you may end up heartbroken and frustrated as the expenses keep rolling in. Look for transparency and clear deliverables.

How do you choose the right Indie publisher?

 KPIs: Identify your success metrics; is it the niche, speed to market, turnkey solutions or author network? Then ask the publisher themselves how they can deliver on that KPI

 Purpose: Indie publishing is a matter of passion; you want to make sure you and your publisher are aligned to each other's passion, purpose and values so you can both enjoy the journey, supporting each other's growth

 Niche: Identify if they have a perfect-fit niche (self-help, for example) and avoid the "we publish anything" type of publishers

Transparency: Is the publisher able to give you a clear list of deliverables? What is included in them, and what is not? Be wary of those who hide a lot more than they reveal. Ask for a clear contract that calls out all terms and conditions, so nothing is a surprise at a later stage

Level of support: Do they provide turn-key solutions, or are they outsourcing suppliers for publishing services? This can make a huge difference in the amount of time you invest and the quality of the publishing experience

System: Do they have a clear system they follow or do they just figure things out? A well-established publisher has systems and procedures in place

Proof of success: You want a publisher that has "done it" rather than one that promises that they "can do it". If they do not have enough success stories, they are probably not very good at what they do

Community: Think about publishers as you would your university; the other authors published by them will become your alumni club. This can make a huge difference to how you get the **ROI** on your book investment

Beyond publishing: What do they do to support their authors beyond getting the book published? Are they invested in the success of the author after the book is published or is this the end of the journey?

I want to share with you the story of Khaled Ismail, an author who went through a similar dilemma when he was trying to zero in on the right kind of publisher. Khaled compiled all his blog posts into a manuscript. He knew it was going to be a great book, but didn't know anything about the publishing process. He took to Google to look for various kinds of publishing and publishers that would take most of the heavy lifting off his shoulders, as he was a working professional who couldn't spend a lot of time on the book. When he approached us, we made sure that his role was confined to the reviews and approvals, and we helped him in every way possible so that his book was published with minimum effort from his side.

For Khaled, the benefits included first-class editing and graphic design that allowed his book to stand out in a sea of competitors. He was also able to access testimonials from other authors who could add to his social proof and his standing on Google. The hard work and sweat of making sure his book was of a high standard was taken on by people who knew what they were doing, and the Passionpreneur imprint on the book meant that it had extra credibility in the eyes of potential readers. Publishing can be confusing and intimidating, but it didn't have to be for Khaled because he partnered with us.

THE BIRD'S EYE VIEW OF THE PUBLISHING JOURNEY

Now that you know how to choose your publisher, it's also important to understand what needs to be done to turn your manuscript into an actual book, even if this work is being done by the publishing team. You'll be better able to ensure quality control of the project and manage your expectations to be more at ease with the process.

Key elements in the journey from the perspective of an Indie publisher:

- Interior of the book
- Book cover
- Launch and handover

In this chapter, we will cover key elements related to what goes inside the book; the other two points will be covered in the following chapters.

 1. **Preparing your content for submission**

 2. **Planning the publishing journey**

 3. **Editing**

 4. **Trim size**

 5. **Typesetting (interior formatting)**

 6. **Final review & approval**

We wil break them down one by one:

 1. Content Preparation

Preparing a proper handover is the key to a smooth publishing journey. So, before you hand over your materials to your publishing manager, make sure you have all your content organised in one folder that includes:

a. **Final manuscript:**
   i. Invest some time in doing a final review of your content before submitting it
   ii. Once the copy-editing process starts, linguistic changes will be acceptable but actual major content changes will complicate the editing process too much (having an impact on quality, deadlines and, potentially, costs)

b. **Bells and whistles:**
   i. Create a sub-folder and put all the items from the bells and whistles in that folder. Keep them in separate documents as they are created

c. **Images, graphs and charts:** These images can be tricky to incorporate into the final version. Each publisher will have guidelines concerning how they should be supplied. Here's what you can do to best facilitate the process:
   i. Make sure to reference their exact location in the manuscript. You do not need to embed them in the document, just reference it in your manuscript with the exact chart name

ii. Ensure that you have the right to utilise the visuals you are using; do not just copy things from the internet. Your publisher might be able to assist in this area. Passionpreneur, for example, provides resources without image-submission guidelines

2. Planning the Publishing Journey

At this point in your author journey, your role switches from creating content to reviewing and approving the product. It still requires proper planning, however, as it encompasses multiple stages over a few months, involving several team members.

The publishing stage is all about refining and packaging your book to have the most impact when it goes out into the world. So, treat it as the start of a new stage in your author journey and approach it with a fresh mind. To ensure that publishing goes smoothly, get in touch with your publishing manager and plan a session with them. The aim here is to understand how the process works and to agree on turnaround times. Both sides need to have clarity on many issues, not least of all a target launch date for your book.

3. Editing

By now you have a manuscript that you believe represents your message. It's time to make it even better. This is where the editing process comes in.

Since you have already used blueprints and worked on your manuscript a couple of times, you might opt for a copy-edit, which aims to polish prose, perfect language, and bring out the best in your narrative voice. Put simply, this is a language review, not a content review, which you would have done before you move to editing.

One or more of the below editing types needs to be done on your manuscript to ensure that your book is linguistically sound:

Content Editing/Structural Editing:

These are essentially two names for the same thing. Content or structural editing addresses the big issues with the manuscript. These include things like structure, coverage, pace and pitch. If you followed the Guided Author system as it was explained then you should not need a structural edit, however if not then a structural edit is highly recommended.

Copy Editing/Line Editing:

Both meaning the same thing interchangeably, typically should be done at no less than 99.9% accuracy guaranteed depending on who you are publishing with.

The big goals of copyediting/line-editing include linguistic correctness, originality and propriety of expression, consistency, fact-checking, formatting, tops and tails (imprint page, illustrations, acknowledgements, and references), and illustration captions.

They cover the detailed checking of the entire manuscript for consistency, accuracy, grammar, spelling, phrasing, and punctuation.

Proofreading:

This occurs after typesetting, and is the final quality control step

- The proofreader checks the manuscript against the stylesheet to ensure editorial decisions have been followed
- Proofreading detects any errors that popped up due to human error in typesetting
- And any errors that were missed during the copy/line edit stage
- They double-check that chapter titles and page numbers in the Table of Contents match those in the body of the book, that the Table of Contents doesn't miss any sections of the book, that page numbers are without mistakes, running heads are correct, and that no new problems arose from typesetting (such as missing words between pages or extra characters popping up at the end of paragraphs).

With the copy and line editing being the first step of any publishing process, it should follow the below steps:

- **Editing sample:** This is an edit of the first 2-3 pages of your book to show you the level of intervention editors are making on your manuscript and to ensure the editing approach matches your style and tone of voice. Make sure you are perfectly happy with it, as this becomes the guideline for the editor to complete the book editing.

- **Round 1 edit:** This will be your full manuscript edited per the agreed style. Editing reviews are done electronically using a "track changes" feature that allows you to accept, modify or reject each suggested edit.
- **Round 2 (final) edit and proofread:** Editors take your feedback and rework the manuscript, then proofread and send it to you for final review and approval. After this, your manuscript will be considered as final.

Now, there are many people who aren't sure what kind of editing is right, or how to go about the whole thing. Not many know that the editing can depend on the genre of the book, as well as the target audience. Let me make it clear for you with an example. Dr Corrie Block made sure his manuscript was free of errors and readable for a non-academic audience. Being a professor, Dr Block has always considered himself a good writer. He'd already published several journal and academic papers. But when it comes to a book and hitting the right chord with the target readership, things are a bit different. Academic readers are used to formal, in-text referencing which can be off-putting to the lay reader. They are also used to technical terms and don't use personal anecdotes and stories to build up the narrative.

It's a transition that can be made quite easily when you know how, and Dr. Block took to it easily when we began working together. We helped him smooth the manuscript and bring out the message in a readable and engaging manner. Soon his rough manuscript was turned into an international book titled *Spartan CEO*, a practical guide for high-performing executives. Dr Corrie even came back to us just one year after publishing *Spartan CEO*, which made him 10x on his investment, and we helped him publish his second book, *Business is Personal*.

 4. Choosing Your Trim Size

Now that we are done with the editing, let's move on to the interior of the book. "Trim size" is the publishing term for book size, measured in inches in a Width x Height format.

The trim size dictates a few things:

- *Page count:* The smaller your trim size, the more pages are required for your content.
- *Global distribution:* If you choose a non-standard trim size, it will be hard to print through the global print-on-demand service and will be difficult to manage logistically.
- *User experience:* Bottom line—it's not about you, it's about your audience. So think about how they will engage with your book and choose your trim size accordingly.

Below is a list of the top recommended sizes with some general guidelines:

- Mass-market paperback: 4.37" x 7" (178 x 111 mm). These are small paperback books. Think of the type sold in airports and supermarkets.
- Inspirational Size: 5"x 8" (203 x 127 mm) used for memoirs, inspirational and spiritual books.
- Digest Size (Industry Standard Size): 5.5" x 8.5" (216 x 140 mm) used for self-help books and business books.
- US Trade Size: 6" x 9" (229 x 152 mm) used for reference books with charts and illustrations.

How do you make a choice? Easy. Just look at other books! Having some real-life examples in your hand should enable you to get a better sense of which trim size is best for your book.

- Go to a bookstore and pull out a few books that get your attention (make sure they're the same genre as yours and not older than two years).
- See how each size looks and feels in your hands.
- Does it look right? Is there too much or too little content on a page?
- Carefully examine the pages and think about how you want to present your content.
- Now place the book back on the shelf. How does it look?
- Also, take note if the cover is matte or glossy.

5. Typesetting

Typesetting is the process of setting text onto a page. At its core, typesetting is about the user experience from the moment the reader picks up the book.

When selecting a typesetting template, consider your target audience and the purpose of the book. Take your time reviewing the provided options and once you do, get your publishing team to create a one-chapter sample to ensure you are perfectly happy with your choice.

Some of the items to consider when choosing your interior design templates:

- **Body Copy Font:** This is the font used in most of your book's text.
- **Title Font:** Also known as "Accent font", this is a more decorative font used for headings and titles in your book.
- **Fleuron:** Also known as a "printer's flower", this is the decorative element used within the book to separate sections within chapters.
- **Font size:** Aside from impacting readability, this also impacts the page count. Using bigger font means more pages, which could be useful in beefing up your book size if you have a low word count.

Keep in mind that the book is meant to cater to the reader's needs, not your taste. Think about the target audience and what key message you want to bring out before making your typesetting choice.

6. Final review and approval

"ARM DOORS AND CROSS-CHECK"

— THE FLIGHT CAPTAIN

When it comes to things that have a drastic impact on your life, you can never double-check enough. That's why the airplane captain gives clear instructions on every single flight to "cross-check". Any failure might cause consequences no one wants to deal with.

The same applies to your book. By now, you have a complete book ready to be published globally; the last thing you want is for your book to come out and then… ouch! you didn't notice something that should have been fixed.

Proofreading is the process of reviewing the book in its final format to ensure consistency and accuracy in grammar, spelling, punctuation and formatting.

Author's Final Proof: After proofreading comes a crucial part of the process. This is when you, the author, print off a copy of your book and check it thoroughly. This is not a time for major changes, but a time when you look for any things that are outside the scope of the proofread – such as content issues, or anything else you might have neglected or forgotten about. Look specifically for things that might change the intended *meaning* of what you have written.

I recommend you find your nearest digital printer and get your book printed and spiral bound, and then take your time to go through it page by page. Be very diligent, so you find any mistakes that might be embarrassing if not fixed. After all, this book is your baby, and you are making sure it is ready to go out into the world.

I can say from experience that this can be an exciting affair; it is the first time you will hold your content as an actual book, so enjoy it.

DON'T RUSH THE BABY

I need to add a word of caution here. The last few weeks before publication can bring a lot of anxiety. It's like a mother in her last month of pregnancy. If this stage is rushed, it will create complications.

A book is no different. To rush is to increase your risk of problems. I see that with many authors who, understandably, become overly anxious about when their book will reach the market. They rush through the last stage only to discover they missed out on something crucial like mentioning someone important in their acknowledgment, misspelling their boss's name or even realising they missed out on adding an important reference. All of these are issues they could resolve before going to print if they took the time to spot them.

I remember this happening with one author in particular who forgot a major acknowledgement in their book. Only when this author held the book in their hands did they find an unpleasant surprise they could have avoided. A moment that should have been so exciting made their heart sink instead. It was an expensive mistake to make because the print run had already been done and the book was already published to many platforms. When your book hits the shelves, you want it to represent who you are and what you bring to the world. You want to make sure you can be proud of this huge achievement!

Contrast this with one of our authors, Maya Mattar. When she did the author's final proof, she read through and realised it didn't reflect who she was after writing the book, or the reality of business at the time she was meant to publish. Why? COVID had hit, her niche market had evolved in major ways to accommodate that, and what was relevant before was no longer valid. She made the choice to halt publication, take a step back and do one more round of corrections, editing and typesetting. Yes, it was a bit of an extra investment, both in terms of time and money, but it was less costly than being disappointed with the final book after printing, losing more time and more money, and most importantly being frustrated rather than proud.

Taking a step back before taking two steps forward was a wise decision by Maya that took courage, humility and discipline. She went from "Maybe it will be an OK book" to "It's a book I'm proud of." She even managed to create a bestseller out of it.

That being said, please be careful not to overdo it. There is a fine line between knowing that you will always grow as a person when going through the book-writing process, and knowing that at some stage you need to publish the book because any more obsessing over it will only reap diminishing returns. Do not get caught in paralysis by analysis. If you find yourself there I say, "Done is better than perfect."

My advice on this is simple: do all the checks. But don't rush the baby. Trust the team to do what they need to do in editing and preparation for publication. If you need something to do, then I suggest you spend that nervous energy planning your launch party (which we will talk about soon)!

The truth is, as much as you don't want to rush your baby, you don't want to delay it either. There is a fine balance here. Do all the checks, but don't rewrite the book. Too much 'analysis paralysis' at the last minute will only make you second-guess the brilliant, hard work you and your team have put in to bring this book into reality. At some point, the book-baby needs to be born.

THINGS THAT COULD DELAY YOUR PUBLISHING JOURNEY

From my experience working with authors, these are the top three issues that cause delays in the publishing journey:

- **Missing deadlines because you are busy:** By now your role is mostly around review and approval; the publisher's team is doing the heavy lifting. Be realistic during the project-planning process given earlier in this chapter, take into consideration all your other commitments and decide what is a realistic pace for you.
- **Rushing the process:** It's interesting to note that attempting to finish things faster could cause you more harm than good. Keep in mind that quality work takes time; rushing this process simply causes more errors, which have time and cost implications. So, take time to think things through before making final decisions, and then allow the team to do good work and exercise quality control.
- **Constantly changing your mind:** By now, so much time and effort has gone into creating your best content. With every stage in publishing, that content becomes even more solid; however, that means the room for changes decreases, since every stage depends on the

ones that came before. Last-minute changes will have an impact on deadlines and the quality of work. They will also affect costs if the change means redoing completed work. Make sure you are investing the time to think things through before you make decisions.

IN SHORT

Publishing is one of the most important stages in your author journey. Although you are no longer burdened with planning your content, typing/recording your manuscript, organising the content and so on, you are making a number of important decisions — editing, typesetting, trim size, etc. — that give shape to your book.

Once you make all the important decisions for the interior of the book, the next step is to work on your book cover, which, in my opinion, is a key factor of a book. That's why I dedicated the whole of the next chapter to it.

 **Well done!
Time to reward yourself.**

9

DO JUDGE A BOOK
BY ITS COVER

First Impressions Last Forever

CHAPTER 9

DO JUDGE A BOOK BY ITS COVER

First Impressions Last Forever

"A PICTURE IS WORTH A THOUSAND WORDS."

YOUR BUSINESS CARD ON STEROIDS

Despite the famous quote "Don't judge a book by its cover," people still do. This is something you cannot avoid, no matter what you do, because people are people.

So, it's important that your book cover be not only relevant to your contents but also eye-catching. The cover is the first thing people see, and it's the one thing that always stands out even if no one opens your book. Remember, the book will be your new business card on steroids, so you really want it to be as impressive as possible.

This is why we have dedicated this whole chapter to the book cover. You will learn about the different aspects that go into creating an impressive cover, starting with the photoshoot and writing the cover brief, through the many other marketing elements impacted by your book cover.

PICTURE OR NO PICTURE?

The first question likely to come to your mind when you think of your book cover is: *Should I put my picture on the front or the back?*

Well, the front is by far the most important element of a book cover. I always recommend that first-time authors have their picture on the front. Remember, your book is your business card until your name is big enough to be recognised. Having your picture helps you get the publicity you need to get there. But, of course, there are exceptions to every rule, so you need to be the judge of what works best for your purpose, message and target audience.

One example of a successful cover with the author's picture on the front is my book *Live Passionately.* This cover was used by the IBPA (Independent Book Publishers Association) as an example of an eye-catching book cover during the preparation webinar for the Frankfurt Book Fair (the world's largest trade fair for books). What worked with this cover was the way my picture said "PASSION" in a larger-than-life way, complemented by the explosive colour splash background. Steve Jeffrey's cover was more dramatic, with a darker colour palette to reflect the title of his book, *Bulletproof Leader.* These were two very different approaches, but similar results in terms of high-quality, eye-catching covers that jump off the shelves.

Both my cover and Steve's cover used our faces as the most recognisable feature. Assile Beydoun and Larissa Redaelli used slightly different approaches. Their covers paired fun and engaging photos of them in combination with other graphic design elements that tied in with their topics. Assile's book, *Lettuce Live Better*, reached Amazon #1 bestseller, and Larissa's book *Happydemic* reached the Amazon Top 100. Both covers leap off the shelf and capture the nature of the book brilliantly.

That is not to say that the only way to get a great cover is to have your picture on the front. On the contrary, there are times where the best option is a very different option. One example is "Flip" by Sadaf Tauqir. This book about giving second chances to yourself and others harnessed eye-catching colours and cutting-edge design to catch the eye of potential readers. It helped cement Sadaf's place as a mindset make-over coach and a thought leader in her niche. Jagdish Kini also used this approach with his book, *Release the Hostage*, and was able to reach Amazon #1 Bestseller in his category.

Essentially, what you need to decide is whether you want or need to use your book cover to establish personal brand recognition. If so, you might want to do what I did. I used my image on the cover of my first book, but not on the following books (including this one). Dr Corrie Block was the same. His face appeared on this first book, *Spartan CEO*, but for his follow-up book, *Business is Personal*, he chose a more sleek and contemporary design as his brand was already established.

EXAMPLES OF BOOK COVERS
WITH AUTHOR PICTURES

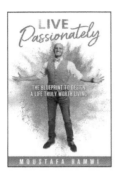

EXAMPLES OF BOOK COVERS
WITHOUT AUTHOR PICTURES

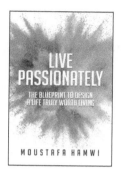

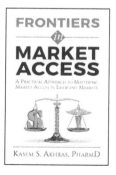

Whatever you decide, you will need an impressive picture to go on the book, front or back. You need to start by planning your photo shoot.

THE MILLION-DOLLAR SMILE

People make judgements about how you look, whether you like it or not.

Is it fair? No.

Is it the reality? Yes.

Why? Because biologically, humans are visual creatures. It's mostly unconscious, but snap judgments of other humans, based solely on physical characteristics and facial expressions, evolved as a way for humans to quickly assess threats and opportunities and to determine the relative status of a new person to know how to interact with them. With that in mind, you want your picture to convey trust, confidence and relevance to your audience.

Even if you do not want to have your picture on the front cover, a photo will be used on the back of the book, for your author page, online marketing, etc. So, you really want to get the best representation of who you are through your photo shoot. It should be as though you can almost speak to your audience through it.

Guidelines to Conducting an Impressive Photoshoot

BEFORE THE SHOOT
Who is your target audience?

....

....

....

Think about the target audience you defined in the strategy session. What are they like? How might they perceive things?

....

....

....

Just remember, different strokes for different folks.
What message do you want to send with the photo?

....

....

....

You say just as much with your appearance as you do with your words. The author photo needs to suggest you are the ideal type of person to be writing about a specific subject. This is your persona, a representation of yourself centred around advertising your work. It is not a complete reflection of you as a person, but only those facets that fit with your work.

How are you going to convey this message?

....

....

....

How much to show: Face only, half body or full body?

....

....

....

Wardrobe: What do you wear? Trying to look appealing to a group of mothers is different from trying to look professional to a group of corporate executives.

....

Body language: Do you want your hands to be showing? How do you want to portray yourself to the audience?

....

....

Facial expressions: Should you be serious or smile? If you smile, is it a cheeky smile, a grin or a million-dollar smile?

....

....

Samples of styles you like:

Have an idea of the style you want on the cover. Browse book covers that you like, not just random photoshoots. A picture that looks amazing by itself might not look great on a book cover (unless you are using it on the back). Share your samples with the photographer.

....

....

THE SHOOT

Bring outfit changes with you:

Photo shoots are expensive, so you'll want to get the most out of a single session. Taking multiple outfits is preferable to having to do reshoots because the bowler hat you thought would make you look like an adorable kook actually makes you look like a weirdo in a bowler hat.

....

....

Styling, hair and makeup:

Ideally, arrange for a professional hair and makeup stylist prior to the shoot (even better if you can get them to join you for the shoot). And gents, do not underestimate the need to get some grooming prior to your session.

....

....

Bring a friend:

If you cannot bring a stylist with you to the session, the next-best thing is a friend. They will help you chill and enjoy the experience. And they will give you some feedback on how you are looking on camera (keep in mind to brief them on what you are looking for, so they do not give too much of their own opinion).

....

....

....

DO JUDGE A BOOK BY ITS COVER

Be natural, be you

All this planning is great. Yet, eventually, during the shoot, people tend to do the things that make them feel most comfortable. So be natural, be you and let your character shine.

And breathe! If you find yourself too tense or unable to get the shots you want, always remember to breathe. I promise you it makes all the difference in the world. A camera tends to make people a little bit too self-aware; breathing brings out the natural flow in us.

....

....

....

....

Enjoy

The most important thing is to enjoy yourself; a shoot takes an average of 30 minutes, so have fun. That is the best way for you to get the best shots and enjoy the process at the same time.

....

....

....

....

BACK COVER CONTENT

"BREVITY IS THE SOUL OF WIT"

— WILLIAM SHAKESPEARE

What the front cover says, visually, the back cover complements in words.

After the title and the front cover, the most important marketing material for your book is the description found on the back, also known as the blurb. It serves your book in the same way a trailer serves a film.

The blurb is the pitch to the reader about why they should buy your book. It is sales copy to get them to see whether the book is for them and make the purchase if it is. This description is used in multiple places other than the back cover. It appears right below the listed price on Amazon, for example; that makes it crucial for this short description to be just right.

So, what's the recommended structure for intriguing back cover content?

 One-liner hook: An inspiring quote, a question to the reader, a shocking statement, or anything that draws the attention of the reader

 About the book: A brief that's between 75-100 words, try using the elevator pitch format below:

- If you are … (describe target audience)
- Struggling with/aspiring to … (describe their pain or aspiration)
- This book helps you to …. (describe what the book helps them achieve)
- Through … (describe how the book helps them)

 About the author: Again, around 75-100 words, this bio is there to establish credibility. Unlike the author bio that goes inside the book, this one needs to be concise. You can talk about achievements or accreditation.

 Credible testimonials: If you have 1-2, as a maximum, very short testimonials, from very credible names, they go here.

Remember to keep it short and sweet. It's an ad, not a synopsis. And in this case, less is more. On average, most Amazon bestsellers have descriptions that are no more than 200 words long.

COVER BRIEF

A good cover depends on a good brief to the designers. A well-written brief ensures that all-important design issues are considered before the designers start work. If *you* are unclear about what you want, then how can you expect someone else who has never met you — and does not know your book — to come up with work that makes you happy?

So, spend time deciding what you want the cover to convey, check out books (online and in-store) and, most importantly, think about your audience and what would resonate with them. Put together a mood board with at least 3-5 book covers you like, and think about what colour palette you want to use; this will become your personal brand's look and feel.

BEYOND THE COVER

Keep in mind that the book cover is part of your marketing kit. It is important to your personal brand to have a consistent look and feel, just as you get from any top corporate. Your marketing kit includes things like:

- Your website/landing page
- Book video promo
- Author card for introducing yourself at events
- Book marketing artwork: customised artwork with your book in 3D to use on social media promotions
- Social media headers: dedicated social media headers with your book image, for use on major social media channels
- Roll-up banner: to use at your live events
- Zoom background with your book cover

Your cover is the face of your book. It is the first thing that anyone will notice about your book, and the *only* thing guaranteed to be seen by everyone, even those who do not read the book. Invest the right level of energy to get the most impressive cover possible. Use this chapter to think carefully about everything that goes into it, from the positioning of your picture all the way to colour palettes and other aspects of the design. And, most importantly, enjoy the process. Book covers are a fun, creative, and strategic project. You are creating your own piece of art.

You are now on the home run towards your book launch, which is what we will discuss in the coming chapter.

Well done!
Time to reward yourself.

ALMOST THERE, KEEP IT UP

The Home Run

CHAPTER 10

ALMOST THERE, KEEP IT UP

The Home Run

*"FINISHING STRONG IS THE ONLY
RESPECTABLE WAY TO FINISH."*

— GARY RYAN BLAIR

Congratulations! You have almost reached the end of your author journey. There are just a few steps left to officially becoming an international author; you've worked hard for it, so keep up the good work to finish strong and get the launch you deserve. In this chapter, we will discuss the last few things left to cross off your checklist, starting with pricing your book, all the way to global distribution setup.

A GOOD HOME RUN

The finishing details make all the difference. To help you finish strong, let's look at some of the key elements we have not tackled yet:

 Pricing your book

ISBN

 Global distribution

 Printing

 Bookstores

 Handover

 Compliance

Let's go through them one by one.

PRICING YOUR BOOK

Pricing is a mental game: it's an art, not a science.

This is particularly true for executives, leaders and entrepreneurs who are focused on using the book as a branding tool, rather than making pennies from book sales.

Consider your goals. Then research similar books in the market before deciding on the best pricing for your book. Here is my personal pricing strategy to help drive more ROI on your book investment: simply price the book as high as possible so you can sell it directly at a discounted price (keep in mind: this *will* impact your online sales, yet as I said earlier, your money is not in the book sales as much as the business you will get from positioning yourself as a global thought leader).

One of the most popular psychological pricing tricks is to end your price in an odd number (e.g. $3.99). Studies have shown that buyers are willing to pay more for something because the price ends in an odd number, like 9 or 5 (the number 9 is the most popular).

Here are some general guidelines on how to go about it.

1. Consider your sales goals:
   - Reach as many readers as possible: Price the same or a few dollars lower than similar books on Amazon.
   - Gain premium positioning: Price higher than average knowing that this will reduce your business to consumer (B2C) sales (this is only good if this fits your target audience).
2. Do some research:
   - Search on Amazon for books similar to yours to get a good idea of where to start pricing your book.
   - Visit your local bookstore and find the section in which your book would be shelved, look at books similar to yours, and check the prices.

3. Decide actual pricing:
    - **Printed book:** Again, depending on your goals, below are some guidelines.

Maximum reach	Balanced positioning	Premium positioning
$9.99 – $13.99	$14.99 – $17.99	$19.99 upwards

   i. Keep in mind to allow enough margin to sell at a discounted price at your events or to corporate clients. For example, if you price at $17.99, you can sell at your event for $15 and to corporates who buy in bulk at $12 or $10.
   ii. *Hardcover books are priced on average 1.5 times more than the aforementioned ranges.*
    - **E-book:** when selling e-books, $3.99 to $4.99 is the perennial favourite.
   i. This price range is popular and therefore comparable to the majority of other e-books. And this price is low-risk for the reader.
   ii. The maximum price you should go for is within the range of $7 less than the print book. So if the print book is selling at $17.99, you can price the e-book at a maximum of $10.99.

Note: *You can have different strategies for print vs. e-book. You can price the print version as balanced, but the e-book cheaper, which is typically the case.*

ISBN

An ISBN (International Standard Book Number) is the book's unique identifier. An ISBN is assigned to each separate edition and variation (except reprintings) of a publication. For example, an e-book, a paperback and a hardcover edition of the same book will each have a different ISBN.

Does an ISBN guarantee your copyright?

This is a tricky question; the answer is yes, but not directly.

The ISBN by itself is not a copyright or trademark registration. However, registering an ISBN proves when you created your content, which in a case of copyright dispute could assist with proving copyright.

Each country has its own rules about acquiring an ISBN, but this will be part of your publisher's work so do not worry about it unless you are self-publishing, in which case you have to do the homework required to figure out the legalities in each country.

 GLOBAL DISTRIBUTION

To enable that "international" element, you need to ensure your book is available across the globe in the most efficient way.

Before I explain how I and my team tackle it at Passionpreneur Publishing, let's look at the concept of Print on Demand (POD).

POD is a printing technology in which book copies (or other documents) are not printed until the company receives an order, allowing the printing of single copies or small quantities. POD books are printed and shipped as soon as someone clicks the "Buy Now" button and completes the purchase. Not a single copy is printed before that, which means there isn't a need for storage to hold thousands of your books.

Think of it as an industrial-scale digital printer for books! Actually, the future is heading towards bookstores having such printers, to save on storage space and be able to print books on demand, on the spot.

Choosing the right POD service is a bit tricky. It mostly depends on what you are trying to achieve. Each solution has its pros and cons. This alone is a topic that could fill a chapter, and it's not necessarily of value to you since, if you go with an indie publisher or even a traditional publisher, they will take care of it. And if you are going the self-publishing route, then you like a bit of DIY and will do your research to find the best solution.

Let me share some insight from my experience. Uploading directly on Amazon might *not* be your best option. Although it has all its obvious advantages, you miss out on being in all other online stores. They all compete with each other. Being native to

Amazon means the rest will not pick up your book. Of course, there are solutions to ensure your book is available across the globe in stores like Barnes & Noble, Apple iBooks, Booktopia, and all major bookstore catalogues. Publishing with a professional publisher, like our own Passionpreneur Publishing, means the publisher takes care of all of that for you.

 **PRINTING**

Yes, the global book distribution game is online, yet printed books have a few advantages:

- The personal joy of holding your "little baby" in your hands
- Using it as a lead generation tool (we will explain this more in the bonus section)
- Displaying them at events and doing book signings after your talk

So, print or not print?

I know that sounds confusing. So let's give you some indications to help you make the right decision:

- For quantities of fewer than 500 copies (say 10, 50 or 100), then your best bet is to utilise a **POD** facility. Just log into your account, enter the address details, make the payment and a few days later, the prints show up at your door.

- For quantities from 500 upwards, you are better off with *offset* printing. The advantage is a cost saving that you get with economies of scale, better quality and more customization, if you have specific finishes in mind (embossing, laminations, spot UV, special paper stock, etc.)

	Offset	**POD**
Pros	• Superior image quality • Better color fidelity • Better paper • Economies of scale	• Faster turnaround time • Cheaper for low-volume jobs • Changing information within a single print job
Cons	• High cost of low-volume • Longer timetable • Worse fallout in case there's an error	• Fewer options in materials • Slightly less color fidelity • Higher cost for large-volume jobs • Slightly lower quality, sharpness and crispness

Again, it's one of the things your publisher should be able to guide you on.

BOOK STORES

Bookstores are a very controversial topic. In most people's mind they're the Holy Grail of being a published author... not in ours!

To start with, one of the big misconceptions is that traditional publishers get *all* their books on the shelves. The reality is that not every book they have in their catalogue gets into every bookstore, because they will prioritise the books they know will get them the maximum sales. Even if your book makes it to the shelves, it could be at a big risk of being taken off the shelves very quickly, unless it sells like hotcakes. This is typically improbable unless your idea is innovative and brand new, you've received great reviews, some influencer is speaking of your book, or you are already a celebrity with a huge following. Retail floor space is simply too expensive to keep unknowns on the shelves for very long.

If you need evidence of what I'm saying, just look around a Virgin Megastore or any major bookstore in your area. You will see that most of them are shrinking their book section and adding stationery, toys, memorabilia and so on.

So, generally speaking, getting your book on shelves is very time-consuming and doesn't have a direct correlation to bringing you measurable ROI. The probability of a senior executive or a key decision-maker of a corporation finding you randomly in a bookstore amongst shelves and shelves of books is remote, even assuming they are looking. They will find you through marketing your book, on relevant social media and your direct outreach. We will discuss more about this in the bonus chapters.

It is still a very nice vanity metric to be able to take a photo of your book on the shelves of a bookstore and show it off to friends and family. There are two main ways to do that:

The first is to go through a book distributor who has access to the bookstore network. They typically go to bookstores pitching multiple books in one go. Obviously, they take a cut on the books sold, but this is probably the most practical way to get your book into bookstores because most bookstores do not deal directly with authors, especially in major metropolitan areas.

The second is to just walk into the bookstore and establish a connection with them; they will guide you on what is needed to get your book on the shelves. Being a local, they would probably want to support you; talk to them about how you can support them, drive traffic and sales and see where this conversation goes. You might have to pull some strings to make it happen if it is really worthwhile for you.

 **HANDOVER**

Do not underestimate the value of a professional handover. I've heard horror stories of authors who worked with unprofessional and self-proclaimed publishers only to find they have no control over their files, or have even had their source material lost. And I had similar experiences before I founded Passionpreneur Publishing.

My first book was published by a self-publisher in the US who was only focused on getting my money rather than providing quality service. A few months after my book was published, I wanted to plan a launch event so needed to access the source files of my cover to make backdrop for the stage. To my shock, the publisher said this is not my property and wanted to charge me close to $1,000 to give me that source file alone! This is still the case until today where I do not have access to the source files of that specific book. This left a bitter taste in my mouth. That's why you need to make sure to ask your publisher to arrange a proper handover of all your files, including:

- **Book files**
  - Cover file
  - Text file: text-only file, ready to print
  - Emailable version: full book (text with cover) for email use
  - Lead magnet: Text with the cover, up to the end of chapter one or two, then the back cover all in one file used as a download on their website to get people to buy the full version
  - Source files: e-pub file should you need to amend the contents of the book

- **Marketing kit**
  Any marketing material that was developed for your book. Having everything in one place makes it easily accessible when you need it, which will happen throughout your launch and after, as you use the book as your promotional tool

With the completion of the handover, you will have full control of your book assets moving forward. Just make sure to keep your files safe so you can access them when needed in the future.

This is a critical point, and is something I was careful to build into Passionpreneur's offering. One of our authors, Dr. Hanan Selim, had the unfortunate experience of writing a full book with a publishing service that did the wrong thing by her. Not only did they not give a full handover of her files, but when she needed them, she couldn't find the files or any way to contact the (presumably defunct) publishing service. She had to start from scratch. Luckily, Dr. Hanan is brilliant, and we were able to help her.

But we also made sure she got all of her files, all of her graphics and add-ons, and that there were no loose ends.

 **COMPLIANCE**

Depending on which market is your home base, there will be some compliance requirements to be taken care of.

- **Pre-approval:** This means you have to submit an application for publishing and distribution approval from something like a ministry of media and information prior to distributing physical books in the country. Examples include UAE and Hong Kong.
- **Public Library Deposit:** This means you send a copy of your book (hard and/or digital) to the government's central public library so they have a record of books published in the country. This is done, for instance, in the US and Australia.

Either way, your publisher should take care of it.

Once all this is done, and your book is listed online for global distribution, you are officially an international author.

But wait…no one knows that — or you — yet!

Don't worry. This is normal. Your book being published and being launched are two different things. Like doing your civil marriage paperwork and having a wedding party (they are not mutually exclusive).

The book launch is the apex of your writing journey, and we have dedicated the next chapter, our first bonus one, to it.

For now, you deserve a BIG CELEBRATION.

 **Well done!
Time to reward yourself.**

BONUS CHAPTERS

*Beyond Publishing, Going
From Author to Authority*

LET THE WORLD KNOW

How to Plan an Effective Book Launch

*"THE KEY TO SUCCESS IS TO
FIND A WAY TO STAND OUT"*

— SETH GODIN

LET THE WORLD KNOW

You figured out your book strategy, have created amazing content and got the bespoke publishing work done. Now, it's time to let the world know.

The great news is that it's not as difficult as you might think. In this bonus chapter, we will go through how to conduct a book launch, one that reaches your target audience and gets you the results you want.

I will show you how to choose the most suitable launch date; we'll look at the must-do arrangements for your launch and then discuss the most efficient ways to get the most from your efforts.

IT'S NOT HOW GOOD YOU ARE, IT'S WHO KNOWS HOW GOOD YOU ARE

In 2018, 1.68 million books were self-published in the US alone.[3] So, the likelihood that your book will automatically be seen by the right audience is not worth betting on.

But you are not trying to compete with those millions of books; you are actually aiming at getting noticed by the people that matter, the target audience we defined in the strategy stage. This is much easier, and more efficient, than just jumping in head-first, hoping to get noticed in a sea of noise.

As with any proper marketing activity, you need to know who you want to speak to, what you want to tell them and where to find them. (You may want to refer back to Chapter 4 that covers strategy, where we looked at these things in depth.) Now it's time to launch using the following three steps:

 1. Re-align with your strategy

 2. Figure out the most efficient way to launch

 3. Choose the best timing for your launch

---

3   https://www.publishersweekly.com/pw/by-topic/industry-news/publisher-news/article/81473-number-of-self-published-titles-jumped-40-in-2018.html

Let's break these down.

 1. Re-align with your strategy: Review your strategy document to be clear about:

- *What* is your primary goal in writing the book?
- Remember, "to become the leading authority on..."
- *Who* must find out about your book for you to be *known* as that authority you want to be?
- *Where* do you find them?
  Figure out where your target audience is (both directly and indirectly). For example, if your audience is corporate HR professionals:
  - <u>Direct</u>: Make a list of the top people you are trying to reach, either in person or by company.
  - <u>Groups</u>: List all the associations these audiences belong to, the conferences they attend, etc.
  - <u>Social media</u>: Most of them will be on LinkedIn, rather than Facebook or Instagram.
  - <u>Other new media</u>: What blogs do they read, what podcasts do they listen to, what websites do they visit, etc.?
  - <u>Traditional media</u>: Think about industry-focused publications.
  - <u>Events and venues</u>: Seminars, conferences, etc.

 2. Figure out the most efficient way to launch: This is how to prepare a launch:

- Prepare your own mailing list.

- Plan activities at relevant events and venues they visit.
  - This could include in-person visits and dedicated book launch events (the latter is my least favourite, as they are very resource-consuming, in terms of both time and money, and generally offer little ROI beyond personal satisfaction).
  - Dedicated marketing activities to capitalise on relevant events and celebrations already happening. This remains one of my personal favourites and can give you a good return on your efforts, with the lowest resources.
- Social media campaign.
  - Announcement posts, running over at least a week. Ideally, you want an announcement to come from your publisher, which is something all professional publishers do. Why do you want them?
    - To give you credibility (which happens when the book is being announced by a known publisher).
    - So you just have to press "share" without having to actually draft each post.
- Direct messages to genuine fans and supporters with whom you have built a relationship.
- PR activities.
  - Press releases: Media is one of the most efficient ways to get your message to the right audience. You can utilise both direct media relations and online releases. Each has its value. The main aim of direct media outreach is qualitative, while online press releases serve the quantity element for Google discoverability purposes.

- Interviews: relevant blogs, podcasts, talk shows, etc.
- Your passion tribe.
  - Friends and family: Send an advance copy at least one month before the launch day and ask them to have an Amazon review ready for the launch
  - Fellow authors: Authors understand authors. If they have already launched, they will know how valuable the support is. And if they have not, they will be more willing to support you (since they too will need your support when their turn comes). Keep in mind that it's a matter of relationships, so you want to have planted the seeds of such a relationship early on in your journey. If you made the right choice of publisher, then this will become a very easy step for you.
  - Genuine fans and followers: I'm not talking about those who simply double-click a social media post and move to the next one. I'm talking about the ones you have some sort of relationship with, even if it's virtual (on email or social media). Those people will be happy to support you because they believe in you.
- Book industry promotion campaigns on Amazon or sites like BookBub and Good Reads. Although I am not personally a big fan of this approach, some authors love to do it. The main reason for my opinion is that you are aiming to build your personal brand with a niche target audience to get high-ticket conversions. Doing Amazon promotions is trying to out-noise the market in a place where you are not even sure your target market is looking.

- Of course, all extra efforts are welcomed. You can even look into email marketing targeted at rented databases, utilising launch partners, fans, supporters, etc.

 ## 3. When to Launch Your Book

"TIMING, PERSEVERANCE, AND TEN YEARS OF TRYING WILL EVENTUALLY MAKE YOU LOOK LIKE AN OVERNIGHT SUCCESS."

— BIZ STONE, CO-FOUNDER OF TWITTER

You have worked so hard for so long to get your book ready; do not be hasty in sending it out into the world. We have seen this happen more than once — the authors rush, jumping on social media to say, "Hey, my book is out!" only to see their post slowly drown in a sea of social media content to be forgotten in no time.

I personally held back on launching my latest book for a few months after it was ready, until I could time it in a way that gave me maximum exposure with the least necessary effort.

Here are a few things to think about before setting your launch date:

- **Special dates:** Are there any relevant dates you can capitalise on?

- Let's say your book is about women empowerment; aim to launch your book around International Women's Day; or
- It could be as simple as launching the book on your birthday, when all eyes are on your social media
- **Major events:** For example, if your book is about the impact of physical health on the performance of a CEO, you can find events that are either:
  - Topic-related: Health and fitness-focused; or
  - Audience-related: Seminars and business functions CEOs are attending
- **Marketing engine readiness:** Do you have everything ready to capitalise on your launch, like your website, landing page, marketing automation engine, etc.?
  - Reach out to the marketing team at your publisher if you have one.

The more you plan your book launch, the more traction you will get, and the more enjoyable the launch will be for you.

The publishing industry standard is 6-12 months' lead time before launching a book. We are not asking you to wait that long, but you will benefit from timing it well, rather than rushing it.

Make sure your book is 100% ready to launch.

- There are lots of things that need to be ready before launching your book. The most important of them is to make sure your book is available on global platforms like Amazon, Kindle, Barnes & Noble, etc. Try ordering your book and see how long it takes to get to you.

• Although it might seem like just a file upload, you will be surprised at how many technical issues occur during this stage. Most of them are out of anyone's control, like a technical glitch on Amazon's end. Sometimes they take many days or even weeks to resolve, simply because of the volume of book uploads such platforms deal with.

One author who did this masterfully was Alaa Elshimy. Not only did Alaa follow the process to the letter in terms of pre-publishing checks, he also timed his book launch to coincide with **GITEX Global. GITEX Global** is a meeting place for some of the world's most influential technology industry names. We are talking over 1,000 expert speakers and 4,000 exhibitors from more than 150 countries. This is a place full to the brim with thought leaders, innovators and people and companies wanting to stay on the cutting edge.

Alaa Elshimy was attending this due to his role as a managing director and senior vice president of a technology-related enterprise. But when he was interviewed for a GITEX-related publication, talk soon focused on his book! This was the perfect marriage of timing and topic, as his book *The Future is Here: Business Transformation for Value Creation* was focused on what tech experts call IR4.0, or the fourth industrial revolution. Usually, the focus of such an interview would be on enterprises, but for Alaa's interview, the focus became his book. This kind of market exposure, at a time and place where people are looking for cutting-edge information to invest in, doesn't happen by accident. It happens with good planning. Alaa made that happen and it gave him unrivaled market positioning among thought leaders and innovators across the world in his field.

Another author who worked the book launch like magic was Hanane Benkhalouk. Her book had already been published, however, she choose to host a launch at Expo 2020 in Dubai. Here, Hanane's tactics were a case study in how to harness the social proof as she got photos and exchanged books with other exhibitors and thought leaders. This had the effect of greatly boosting her visibility. She even got a photo with Sheryl Sandberg — author of *Lean In*, COO of Facebook and one of *Fortune* Magazine's most powerful women in business. What an opportunity! For Hanane, waiting to hold the launch paid off big time.

IT ISN'T OVER YET

A book launch is a collaborative effort between you, your publisher and your passion tribe. And although the launch is a celebration date, book promotion is an ongoing effort rather than just a sprint.

So, aim to be a sniper instead of using a "spray and pray" approach. This is true even when you have a lot of resources — you are starting the journey of building your personal brand and using that to grow your business. You should be aiming to use your passion to dominate your market; so, as a bonus chapter, I have decided to give you some insight into how to dominate your market niche. That's what the next chapter is about.

THE BLUEPRINT FOR DOMINATING YOUR MARKET NICHE

From Author to Global Thought Leader

"THERE IS NO PASSION TO BE FOUND
PLAYING SMALL — IN SETTLING FOR A LIFE
THAT IS LESS THAN THE ONE YOU ARE
CAPABLE OF LIVING."

— NELSON MANDELA

WELCOME TO A NEW ERA IN YOUR LIFE

First of all, I cannot say it enough… well done!

You have succeeded where most people have failed, finishing your book and becoming an international author. That, by itself, is an achievement of a lifetime, and it puts you in a different league from most people — which means you also have to play a different game than most people play.

One of the most satisfying parts of my work at Passionpreneur Publishing is coaching my authors on how to use their book as a tool to dominate their market niche. I share with them a kind of roadmap to getting return on their investment and positioning themselves as a global thought leader. In this bonus chapter, I will give you a bird's-eye view of that roadmap.

WELCOME TO THE SHARK TANK

For most people attempting to write a book, the goal is to get the book done. Once that goal is reached, the glass ceiling of self-limiting beliefs is shattered. For a while after the book launch, being an international author made me feel like I was finally the big fish … that is until I realised that my competition had changed. I was no longer competing with the average semi-pros: I was up against everyone else who was an international author, people who had years of experience in playing the pro game.

It felt like I had stepped out of a small pond into an ocean full of sharks. It freaked me out at first, but I got excited when I thought of all the opportunities waiting for me.

Aligned with my passion for leaving a legacy and having access to a lot of the world's top mentors, I simply rolled up my sleeves and dove into researching how the pro game works. A light-bulb moment for me was realising that, although there is money to be made when you are truly a bestselling author, this is a long game to play.

In most cases, creating a true international bestseller is a matter of years and multiple books. Dr Marshall Goldsmith said this about his recent book, *Triggers*, which got him a $1.4 million advance from the publisher before he even wrote it: "I wrote 33 books and finally somebody bought one."

Obviously, this is a joke, since *Triggers* was his third New York Times bestseller, but three bestsellers out of 33 books over 33 years gives you an indication of how tough the book sales game is. Another example is *The Monk Who Sold His Ferrari* by Robin Sharma. The book was originally self-published by Robin, then picked up by HarperCollins Publishing in 1997, but it took years of marketing before it actually became a global phenomenon around 2013. (Think of when you heard about Robin Sharma first. It was probably no earlier than 2013.)

However, international authors like Dr Marshall, Robin Sharma and Brian Tracy now command speaking fees in the range of $60,000 – $100,000 and coaching fees in the hundreds of thousands. Best of all, this revenue is made in the short term, instead of waiting for years; and, unlike with book sales, the speaker gets the majority of the income. (Even if you go for hybrid or self-publishing, Amazon will take about half the money you make from book sales.) In speaking or coaching, you only pay a small percentage to the speaker bureau representing you, and this is only for gigs they get you.

So, I made a major shift from focusing on marketing the book to using the book to market me. I stopped worrying about book sales and started using the book as a lead-generation tool.

Bearing this in mind, here are some of the main uses for your book:

- Brand-building to position yourself as *the* thought leader in your field, against your competition
- Finding potential clients, especially those who might be hard to reach
- Increasing your conversion rate
- Raising your fees

Let me give you an example here. When I started my speaking and coaching career, I was almost begging just to get on stage, even for free, to get exposure.

After publishing my first book, I started using it as my business card when meeting new clients considering me for a speaking gig at their event. In a span of about six months, I went from struggling to get paid speaking gigs to charging $1,000, then $2,000 and then $3,000 per speaking engagement. And my conversion easily tripled; I went from converting around 1 out of 10 to more like 30-40%.

By the time I published my second book, my speaking fees went up to $10,000, with a consistent flow of inquiries for my speaking services and a majority of the leads converting into a consistent flow.

THE ROADMAP

From what you have read so far, you can see that writing a book is the beginning of the journey, not the end. Gaining a global thought-leader position is your Everest.

Is it going to be hard? Hell, yeah!

But is it worth it? 100%. Especially if you are true to your purpose of playing to the best of your abilities. Remember, you will save a lot of energy on such an adventure if you have a clear roadmap — like writing your book using the Guided Author methodology.

Such a roadmap is an extensive discussion that needs a book by itself, and it requires ongoing coaching like my authors at Passionpreneur Publishing receive. But I really want to help you kick-start that journey, so here are the most important things for you to work on:

- Your mission is to inspire, inform and instruct your clients — to get them from where they are to where they want to be.

- Money is only made through a trade transaction (regardless of what the product or service is). Even if you are not in this for the money, running a successful business requires money, so, you want to be able to generate at least enough to keep your enterprise running.
- In the long run, you want to move away from the "hours for dollars" model because it is not scalable. No matter how high your fees, there are only so many hours in the day, and you are a human who is bound to deal with health issues, family issues, etc.
- You are in the business of providing knowledge products or services that are value-added offerings dependent on your experience and that have clear deliverables.

Now that we are on the same page about what it is you actually need to do, let's talk about how to use your book to dominate your market niche.

 1. Find your niche and write a book around it

 2. Productise your book

 3. Create your digital footprint

 4. Create automation systems

5. Identify your hit list and pitch to them

Let's break down each of these ideas.

 1. *Find your niche and write a book around it:* Although this is something you have already done, I would urge you to go back to the drawing board and start refining it further. You are a different person now than when you began your writing journey. You have a lot more knowledge, so your way of looking at things is totally different, especially after reading this chapter. Survey your ideal clients for any insights you might have missed and understand what they are willing to pay you for. It is also important to research your competition (the big sharks, not the small fry. You are swimming in the ocean, not the pond now).

 2. *Productise your book:* If you used the Guided Author System I showed you in this book, then it's your lucky day, because the way the blueprint system was created already takes this step into consideration. Your book can easily be converted into:
- Blogs/content pieces for marketing use
- A simple guide/"how-to" roadmap
- Industry reports/white papers
- Self-study material
- Webinars/online summits

- Audio programs
- Online courses
- Video/new media
- Talks/speeches
- Workshops/seminars
- Consulting/coaching manuals
- Certification programs
- Mastermind/group coaching
- Other products

Get creative and see what you can come up with.

As you can see, the possibilities are endless. Most global thought leaders have all of these products. However, you want to start by focusing on the top 2-3 that your clients are willing to pay you for, and from there you can slowly build your empire.

 3. *Digital footprint:* To be clear, I am not talking about just a website here, I'm talking about a well-structured, fully-fledged digital footprint, which is something that requires investments of time and money. You might be thinking that I am complicating your life by telling you to make new investments and start new projects, but there are more advantages to it than you think.

<u>The world is digital</u>: The world is already more digital than you think, especially for thought leaders, who are, by nature, knowledge-product providers like you

and me. By the time the global pandemic hit in early 2020, my business was already fully digitized, so I felt only negligible negative impact while others were drowning.

<u>Measurable ROI</u>: Digital gives you the ability to measure the efficiency of your efforts. You can simply track your client journey from the minute they download your lead magnet, throughout their content-marketing journey, all the way till they pay for your services.

<u>Targeting</u>: Focusing on your niche is the only way to optimise your resources. In addition, digital means you can target people based on behaviour, preferences, and purchase history, so that you can send the right message to the right people at the right time.

<u>Speed to market</u>: You can simply find your client, launch a campaign and engage with them faster than via any other media in history.

 4. *Marketing Automation:* In simple terms, marketing automation is the use of software that eliminates repetitive marketing tasks. Most of my business is fully automated. This includes, for example, managing my calendar, so I no longer need a PA to manage my appointments; email marketing, where the system sends different emails to potential clients based on their behaviour towards the previous email; online

proposals, for which I can track how many minutes a person spent on a page; and online contracting, where online signatures generate automatic updates of client info to our invoicing system, which sends them the relevant link to pay online.

Just imagine how many people were traditionally needed to manage such tasks; and how much money and headache this would cost if you had to do it the old-school way. Such automation tools work for social media and content marketing, too, which are going to require consistent effort from you to gain thought-leader positioning.

 5. *Identify your hit-list:* Now that you have the full system in place, all you need is a hit list of ideal clients (which you have already defined in the strategy stage of writing your book and refined in the earlier steps of this chapter) and then you can start reaching out to them with your offer.

Once you have everything ready, you are well on your way to dominating your market niche.

YOU'VE GOT THE RECIPE, NOW MAKE IT YOURS

When we talk about dominating your market niche, there are a few names that spring to mind instantly from the many amazing authors I've had the pleasure of working with. The first is Mohanad Alwadiya. His book, *Landlording*, sold 90,000 copies in its first year and became an Amazon #1 bestseller. But Mohanad has always said that this book was his business card. He used it to open doors. When you look at his visibility in Dubai and across the world now, it is undeniable. He is known as the Wolf of Real Estate, but the book is an addition to his business, TV appearances, and other media appearances. He has taken the "Author = Authority" literally. That kind of success story excites me, because passionate thought leaders are the people I set out to work with!

A second name is that of Anthony Joseph. Anthony is a self-made "serial entrepreneur" who was born in the USA, raised in Lebanon and moved to Dubai eight years ago with just a few hundred dollars in his pocket. When he began writing his book, *Take Charge*, through Passionpreneur, I just knew he would do just that. He was going to use this book to open doors and dominate his niche. It started with strategy, and he followed it right through to launch and beyond. Today, he is also an Amazon #1 bestseller who helps aspiring entrepreneurs achieve their goals. He also hosts a popular podcast and is positioned as a highly visible, very successful man in the real estate scene in Dubai.

The final name I'll mention, although the success stories are many, is that of Sarah Tabet. She could have become another HR writer lost in a sea of HR writers. But right from the beginning she took her strategy and niche seriously. What was she good at? What was she passionate about? What were people looking for and willing to pay for? This resulted in her very specific niche becoming clear — inclusion. When her book was published, Sarah began to emerge as a thought leader in a specific area of HR. She had visibility! She began to be seen as a thought-leader globally and was even interviewed by bestselling author and women's leader, Sally Helgesen. Sarah continues to build on this amazing work. She's not just a first time author. She's a globally known name in her field.

It is with people like Mohanad, Sarah and Anthony in mind that the whole Guided Author System has been set up. That strategy session, finding your specific niche, is what starts it off. Everything else along the way builds on that, clarifies and expands on it, until you have a book in your hands that can open the door to dominating your market niche.

SUCCESS IS A JOURNEY, NOT A DESTINATION

This chapter has given you a bird's-eye view of the roadmap our authors use to dominate their market niche. Of course, becoming a global thought leader is not only about sales and marketing. You will have to do a lot of other non-metric stuff and off-line/in-person activities, such as speaking at events, engaging with local groups and communities, conducting PR and media campaigns and supporting causes.

That being said, my logic for focusing on sales and marketing first is simple: if you are not converting all your publicity into actual paying clients, then there is something wrong in the system you built; you are just another "social media influencer".

So, going for anything less than dominating your niche means you are not playing to the best of your abilities, especially after becoming an international author. The topic of thought leadership and dominating your market requires a book in itself, and I am looking forward to writing it.

CONCLUSION

 ## DONE IS BETTER THAN PERFECT!

Firstly, the last words I will say is WELL DONE for reaching so far.

I'm proud of you for finishing this book, that is your first step in joining the Passionpreneur Tribe with the purpose to help inspiring leaders share their message with the world and become global thought leaders. Through this, we collectively spread passion and purpose in the world through a global Passionpreneur network.

You know how we talked about courage, humility, and discipline? You have demonstrated all three by completing the reading of this book. What you need now is renewed discipline to finish writing yours.

Your next step is to turn your experiences into a bestselling book using what you learned here. Do not make it perfect; I always say to our authors "done is better than perfect". You are only going to get better as author by writing a book after a book, so just put a deadline to finish your first one and get on with it.

The last thing I will leave you with is this: this book, *The Guided Author* was concluded one week after my father passed away. What's your excuse?

Always remember:

You have a message to share.

The world is waiting for your book.

Moustafa Hamwi
CEO and Founder Passionpreneur Publishing

 Well done!
Time to reward yourself.

WANT HELP IN BECOMING A GLOBAL THOUGHT LEADER?

We Can Make it Happen

ABOUT THE AUTHOR

Moustafa Hamwi

Award-winning author, speaker, and executive coach.

CEO and Founder of Passionpreneur Publishing.

Moustafa is considered to be one of the world's top experts on the use of passion to spark creativity, entice innovation, and awaken the entrepreneurial spirit of a true leader.

He popularised the term "Author = authority", a phrase which has awaked a passion for authorship in countless thought leaders and helped them transform their intellectual capital into something that they can leverage for business growth.

He was named one of the top 100 leaders of the future by the world's #1 Executive Coach, Dr Marshall Goldsmith, and he was nicknamed Mr Passion by Prof. Tony Buzan, inventor of mind mapping.

Moustafa's philosophy is to live life so fully that it becomes a life worth dying for. He is on a mission to **help inspiring leaders like you share their message with the world and become global thought leaders**. The global Passionpreneur network will collectively spread passion and purpose in the world.

Go to www.Moustafa.com for more information on how to **IGNITE PASSION** so you can win the game of work and the business of life.

Go to www.PassionpreneurPublishing.com for more info on how you can become an international author in 3-6 months.

GO GLOBAL

WANT TO BECOME A GLOBAL THOUGHT LEADER?

You spent years becoming the best in your industry; NOW is the time to become a global **thought leader.**

Moustafa's mentoring and methodology helped experts become positioned as global thought leaders so they can stand out in a room of their peers, build a business around their passion and charge what they are worth. His success has been acknowledged by global industry leaders or as quoted by one of the top leadership coaches in Asia, "Moustafa achieved in 1 year what took others 20 years in this industry to achieve."

Reach out if you want help you to get recognised as the 'go-to' authority in your niche, to monetise your personal brand, and to attract more of your ideal clients – that is, to DOMINATE YOUR MARKET.

If you are a **PROFESSIONAL EXPERT** (Executive, Entrepreneur, Coach, Speaker), we help you **GET RECOGNISED AS A GLOBAL THOUGHT LEADER** by helping you find your niche, publish your book in three to six months, and build your influencer site.

OR,

if you are **ALREADY AN AUTHORITY IN YOUR FIELD** and have a **CONSIDERABLE FOLLOWING,** we help you **MONETISE YOUR BRAND** through consulting and done-for-you services that create your product offers, build your sales funnels, and help you pitch to your audience from the stage.

Get in touch directly with our Passion Assistant on pa@moustafa.com for more information on how to become the 'go-to' authority in your niche.

NOTES

Lightning Source UK Ltd.
Milton Keynes UK
UKHW030629200922
409139UK00001B/162